Emily Post's Teen Etiquette

Emily Post's

Teen Etiquette

ELIZABETH L. POST and JOAN M. COLES

HarperPerennial

A Division of HarperCollinsPublishers

FIRST EDITION

Designed by Nancy Singer
Illustrated by Mari Estrella

Library of Congress Cataloging-in-Publication Data

Post, Elizabeth L.
    [Teen Etiquette]
    Emily Post's teen etiquette / Elizabeth L. Post and Joan M. Coles. — 1st ed.
       p.   cm.
    Rev. ed. of : Emily Post talks with teens about manners and etiquette
    Includes index.
    ISBN 0-06-273337-0
    1. Etiquette for children and teenagers.   I. Coles, Joan M. II. Post, Elizabeth L.   Emily Post talks with teens about manners and etiquette.   III. Title.
BJ1857.C5P62   1995
395'.123—dc20   95-18503

96 97 98 99 ❖/RRD 10 9 8 7 6

A Word from the Authors

I wish to dedicate my work on this book to my grandchildren, Casey, Caroline, Nick, Jeep, Paul, Peter, Danny, Willy, Anna, and Liz, some of whom are, and some of whom will be, old enough to enjoy it and benefit from it.

Elizabeth L. Post

My work on this book would not have been possible without the help and guidance of many important people, but most especially my family: Lillian and A.B. Myers, my parents, who instilled important values and codes of conduct that have served me well; Ashley and Preston, my children, who endured, and then politely ignored, my numerous etiquette lectures, but who also provided inspiration and encouragement along the way; Chet, my husband, who loves me and who *always* encourages me, even though it is *not* always to his advantage to do so!

Joan M. Coles

CONTENTS

CONTENTS

INTRODUCTION

Good for you! The fact that you are reading this book right now is an indication that you are curious and open-minded enough to see what it might have to offer you. You are obviously someone who wishes to better yourself, to know how you can get along better in your world. We can help. We've written this basic book to cover situations you're most likely to confront.

How many times lately have you felt unsure of yourself? Have there been times when you wished you knew what was expected of you, how you were supposed to act, what you were expected to say or do? It happens a lot during the teen years. Even the most popular guy or girl feels insecure at times.

It's possible to fake confidence, to pretend that you're cool, that you know what to do, that you're in control. But faking it never feels right—and you spend a lot of time worrying that you'll be exposed. Compare that feeling to how it feels to have studied hard for a test, ace it, and know you did a good job. That's genuine confidence.

It is our hope that through the information presented in this book, you will be prepared for any social situation. Etiquette provides the knowledge, and gives you the confidence you need, to pass the test of life.

FAMILY AND HOME LIFE

It has often been said, "Manners begin at home." It's true—and they begin with you. No matter how hard your parents may have tried to drill good manners into you, you will not make manners a part of your life until you realize the importance of kindness and courtesy toward others.

Consideration for Others

You probably figured out as a child that you got more of what you wanted when you smiled, or said please and thank you. Now that you are a teen, however, more is expected of you. Those bad table manners that your family let slide may now embarrass you in front of your friends or their parents. Now you're expected to meet and make conversation with a date's parents or a prospective employer, but no one has ever really taught you how to make conversation with an adult you wish to impress. You can do it! Just remember that etiquette is basically common sense and thoughtful behavior. The rules of etiquette provide you with guidelines on how to act in almost every situation involving contact with other people. They provide a bridge between you and your parents, you and your friends, and between your childhood and your adulthood.

Parents

Whether you live with one or both parents, stepparents, grandparents, foster parents, or adoptive parents, your family and your home (good or bad) are a big part of your world. Have you thought about what you can do to make your relationship with your parents better, or do you just blame your parents for all your troubles? Sometimes to get, you gotta give! Try a few of our tips and see if they help.

Communicate
If your parents seem "out of it," it may be because you've left them out. Clue them in to what's going on with you in your life, and pay attention to what's going on in theirs. Notice that the times they seem unreasonable are probably the times they are preoccupied with their own troubles, or when they don't feel they have enough information about a situation, or don't understand it well enough to make a decision. If you feel that your parents have treated

you unfairly, or that you have been misunderstood, talk about it.

Frankness and communication are vital to family harmony. If you have something on your mind, speak up! Often your parents are wondering why you've been moping around the house for days. . . and they may be relieved to hear that the only thing bothering you is that you need a raise in your allowance. The reverse is also true. If your Dad has been on edge lately, ask him if it's something you've done or failed to do. You may be relieved to hear that his stress has to do with something outside the home—perhaps the loss of an important sale at the office.

Airing problems remains the best way to solve or at least diminish them.

TALK ABOUT IT

Something on your mind?
Need to talk about it?
Not sure how?

Choose your time carefully. People are more inclined to listen if you approach them at a time when they are not otherwise occupied. If you're having trouble finding a time when your Dad is free to talk with you, make an appointment. Say something like, "Dad, we need to talk. When would be a good time?" When it is important to you, don't be put off

TALK ABOUT IT
(Continued)

by a casual response. If Dad says he can talk "later," then ask a follow-up question: "OK, Dad, I'll be home from basketball practice at 8:30 tonight. Can we talk then?" Your willingness to pursue an issue is a sign of growing maturity that may come as a pleasant surprise to your parents.

Choose your words carefully. Always begin your comments with "I" rather than "You." Statements such as, "I am angry that I can't go to the party next week. I've agreed to my regular curfew rather than asking for a later one. My friend's parents will be home. I don't understand what your concern is. I feel like you don't trust me," is more effective and makes your listener less defensive than, "You are being *so* unreasonable. All the other parents are letting their kids go to the party next week. What's the matter with you?"

Mention your feelings. Did you notice that the above statements not only began with "I" but also included an expression of what you were feeling? When someone else understands your feelings, it may change the way they view the situation and once in a while even affect the outcome. Perhaps you aren't allowed to go to

---

TALK ABOUT IT
(Continued)

the party because your parents made plans that require you to babysit that night. Once they understand how you feel, maybe they'll offer to hire a babysitter instead.

Keep an open mind. In spite of your best efforts to remain calm and communicate your feelings clearly and honestly, you may not always get the outcome you want. Your parents still may not let you go to the party. Try to be as open to, and considerate of, their feelings and concerns as you want them to be about yours.

Get Organized

You've probably noticed that things run more smoothly when you are organized. Nevertheless, you don't always feel like being organized. If you want to reduce conflict with your family, though, a little advance planning does help.

Plan Ahead

Your parents may be more willing and able to get the materials you need for a special project, drive you to a special function, or plan a special meal if you let them know further in advance than the night before that there's a report due on Thursday, a party on Friday, and a friend coming over on

Saturday. Maybe a weekly "scheduling" meeting with your parents would help. Or even a family calendar hanging in the kitchen.

Cooperate

The best thing about cooperation is that it goes both ways. If your Dad makes a lot of phone calls for business at night, negotiate times when the phone is available to you. But if you come home from school and use your computer modem to cruise the Internet for a couple of hours, remember that someone else in the family may need to use the phone while you're tying it up. You may also need to negotiate the times you want to use the television, VCR, or sound system, or even the times you simply want to be alone for whatever reason: homework, writing in your journal, quiet reflection, or an uninterrupted shower.

When Parents Work

There was a time when almost every family was headed by two adults who were married to each other. The husband and father worked outside the home, and the wife and mother stayed home to raise their children. Some families are still like that, but many others are not. You may be living with a single parent, a parent and a stepparent, a relative, or dividing your time between parents. Because of such living arrangements, and because in many families both parents work, you may have to take responsibility for yourself and help out running your household.

Enjoy Your Time Alone

If your parents' work means a lot of alone time for you, rather than feeling sorry for yourself use your time alone to enjoy a hobby, get a head start on the homework, or listen to your favorite music really loud! (But be considerate of your neighbors if you live in close quarters.)

Help Out With the Housework

Every teen needs some "down" time—time spent doing something relaxing or to chill out and do nothing at all. Adults need down time, too. When your parents work and you are in school, no one has time to do *all* the chores. But if each person does a few, then everyone has time to relax. Pick some of the chores you don't mind, and volunteer to do those.

Pick Up After Yourself

You'd be surprised what a difference it makes—in your parents' mood and in the appearance of the house. Put your dirty clothes and towels in the hamper, wash (or put in the dishwasher) the dishes you dirty throughout the day, pick up messes you make in the family room, kitchen, and bath.

Take Safety Seriously

When you're away from home. . .

> *Always carry money for a phone call.* If you lose your key, miss your bus, or have car trouble,

you'll be able to call someone to help you.

Hide your house key in an unlikely place or take it with you. Hiding it under the doormat, in the mailbox, or on a nail in the garage is too obvious. See if you can think of a place no one would ever think to look, preferably some distance from the door. Or consider leaving a key with a neighbor who's home all day, for emergencies.

Don't accept rides from strangers. I know your parents have been telling you this since you were old enough to cross the street: No matter how nice someone may seem, if you don't know them—don't get in the car. Kids have been raped or murdered by someone who claimed to be a friend of a friend, or a friend of their parents. If you drive and have car trouble, put on your emergency flasher and lock your doors. Ask any-one who stops to call the police for you. It's a good idea to carry a "Call Police" sign for your back window in times of trouble. Call your police department for details.

When you return home. . .

Pick up the mail and newspaper. For safety's sake, you want your house to look occupied. Open only the mail that is addressed to you and put the rest in the same place every day so your parents will know where to find it.

Don't go into your house or apartment if some-

thing looks suspicious. If the door is ajar or something looks strange to you, go to a neighbor's house and call your parents for advice. If you're unable to reach them, call the police. Don't worry about looking silly or being scared.

Make a habit of keeping the door locked all the time. Whether you're home alone or the whole family is present, keep all the doors locked. Even if you leave "for just a minute," lock it.

Let your parents know every time you leave home. Leave a note or call them at work (whichever they prefer), to let them know where you are going and when you expect to return, every time you leave the house. Even if you think you'll be back before they get home, a "short" visit may become a long one, and your parents will be very worried if they don't know where you are.

Never open your door to strangers. Get your parents to install a peephole if you don't have one. You must be able to see who is at the door. If you don't recognize them, even if they claim to be a repairman or that your parents sent them, don't let them in. Give them a specific time to come back when you know your parents will be home. If the person doesn't go away, call the police. Don't feel dumb or rude about not letting someone in. It's better to be safe than sorry.

Don't take medication when you're home alone

unless your parents instruct you to. If you're alone and you don't feel well, call one of your parents or an adult you trust. Follow their directions. If you get worse, call again. If you feel so bad that you really don't want to be home alone, tell your parents or ask someone to stay with you.

Keep a list of important telephone numbers near the phone. These should include your parents' work numbers, relatives' and neighbors' phone numbers, emergency, medical, and fire department numbers, as well as the numbers of some of your friends. The list should always be kept in the same place so that you can find it when you need it. If your phone can be programmed to automatically dial certain numbers, use that feature to store your parents' work numbers and the numbers for emergency assistance.

Brothers and Sisters

The fact that siblings live under the same roof and can't avoid each other doesn't mean they always like each other. Your feelings toward one another may change from day to day. But however you feel, if you recognize that your brothers and sisters are individuals with just as many problems as you, that their likes and dislikes may not be similar to yours, and that they have the right to share your parents' affections, family relations will run much more smoothly.

With your siblings, try to. . .

Avoid jealousy. It's not easy when your sister has gorgeous blond hair and is a real guy magnet, or your brother is the star on every athletic team and you feel like a klutz all the time. Maybe your parents are even guilty of comparing you to your sibling. Don't you make those kinds of comparisons. You're different from your brother or sister, so why shouldn't you look and act differently? It would probably surprise you to learn that star athlete brother of yours is secretly proud of the article you wrote for the school newspaper. Of course, he'd never tell *you* that. Think about your piercing blue eyes, or your ability to play the guitar. If you can realize or develop your own assets, you won't be threatened by the looks and actions of your brother or sister, or anyone else.

Respect privacy. Diaries, journals, and letters are personal. They may never be opened or read without the owner's permission, nor may you listen in on private phone calls. If you even think about it—stop for a minute and think about the reverse: how you'd feel if your sibling read your private thoughts or listened to your phone call.

Remember, too, that a closed door is a request for privacy. If you need alone time, close—but for safety's sake, don't lock—your door. If you must enter a closed room, knock and wait to be admitted before opening the door.

Know when to tell and when not to—but that's easier said than done! Don't tell just to get your sibling in trouble, or to make yourself look good. Do tell when your brother or sister is doing something that is harmful to themselves or others, is dangerous, or is against the law.

Guests in Your Home

Your Guests

When your good friends from school or the neighborhood drop by, you probably treat them pretty much like family. Remember, though, that they are guests in your home. Do what you can to make a good friend feel comfortable. It's polite to offer a beverage or snack, especially if you're having something.

Overnight guests probably need a little coaching on some of your family routines, such as "We always leave the bathroom light on overnight," or "Mom likes to sleep in on Saturdays, so we can't watch TV or play our boom boxes before nine."

Special guests, such as a date, teacher, or new friend, will not be as familiar with your home and family and will appreciate some guidance from you. Always introduce a new friend to your parents. Ask your guest to sit down and offer some refreshment. If he refuses, don't insist. The length of the visit depends upon its purpose. If you sense that your guest is ready to leave but is unsure how to do so, stand up and say something like, "I'm so glad you dropped by. I hope you'll come by again some time soon."

Your Parents' Guests

You probably take for granted adult neighbors and family friends that visit your home often. Even though you may see them a lot or know them well, you should always greet them warmly when they visit. A smile and a handshake, or hug if you know them well, is never inappropriate. If you're invited to join the adult conversation, do so if you like. Be careful, though, not to intrude into what appears to be a private conversation.

From time to time, you may need to greet an adult guest of your parent in a more formal way. Perhaps a business associate drops by, or maybe your divorced Mom or Dad's date for the evening wishes to meet you. Under such circumstances, you are expected to stand when he or she enters the room, smile, shake hands, and make a few minutes of polite conversation. If there is a TV or radio playing, turn it down until your parent and guest leave the room, or excuse yourself and go to another part of the house.

Household Help

Anyone working for your family—a housekeeper, cook, gardener, or plumber—deserves to be treated with respect and consideration. Presumably your parents have outlined their duties. You may ask, politely, for an occasional favor such as getting a shirt or blouse ironed, but don't add a lot of extra chores to their regular duties, and don't ever give orders yourself.

If you are old enough to be living in an apartment, dormitory, sorority or fraternity house, the same guidelines apply to anyone working there who has been hired, or is being paid by, someone other than yourself.

Roommates

Whether you share your bedroom at home with a sibling, or a dorm room or apartment with a friend, consideration of the other person's possessions and space is of the utmost importance. We knew of two sisters who shared a room and decided the way to handle their disagreements was to draw a line down the center of the room which neither of them would cross. The only problem was that one sister's half of the room contained their mutual closet, and the other sister's half had the entrance to the bathroom. Needless to say, the solution caused more problems than it solved.

Sharing Possessions

Living with another person does require compromise. Dividing storage space, negotiating phone, radio, and TV use, establishing a neatness standard, and agreeing not to borrow each other's things without permission can prevent a number of problems. Certain things warrant further discussion:

Common Rooms

Family room. After you and/or your friends have used the family rooms, it is up to you to throw out soft drink containers and snack bags, to pick up magazines, cards, videogame cartridges, and books, to take dirty dishes to the kitchen, and generally to leave the room ready for the next person.

Kitchen. Kitchen rules should be negotiated with your parents or roommates. Check before consuming food that looks as if it might be intended for a special meal. Rinse and stack your dirty dishes in the sink—or better yet, wash them or put them in the dishwasher. It takes only a minute or two to take care of your own mess, but it takes much longer for one person to clean up after everyone.

Bathroom. Sharing a bathroom can also put a strain on people living together. Finding wet towels on the floor, a ring around the bathtub, and a toothpaste tube that's been squeezed in the middle can be infuriating! Not to mention when someone hogs the bathroom for hours on end. You may have to schedule bath times and cleanup. But you'll never go wrong if you leave the bathroom tidy.

Appliances

Washer and dryer. If you're responsible for the family laundry or simply your own, be sure you know how to use the machines before attempting to do a load. Promptly transfer wet clothes to the dryer. Remove and fold clothes as soon as they're dry to prevent excess wrinkles.

Microwave and refrigerator. Just be considerate. Clean up your mess and don't eat anything that you know someone else is saving for later.

Dishwasher. If in doubt, use less rather than more soap. Too much soap can cause problems to the dishwasher or the dishes. Everyone has a favorite method for loading the dishwasher. Rinse your dishes, and try to place items in the appropriate basket or rack.

Electronic Equipment

Computer, TV, VCR, and sound systems. Expensive equipment is often shared by a number of people. Obviously, don't fool with a complicated system unless you know how to use it. Negotiate use times with family or roommates. Remember, too, to keep the sound at a level that is considerate of others. Earphones can solve the noise pollution, but wearing them for extended periods of time at high volume can damage your eardrums. Be sure to return tapes and discs to their storage containers when you are finished.

Cameras, cellular phones, and other portable equipment. Handheld electronic equipment such as 35-mm cameras, video cameras, electronic games, audiotape or compact-disc players, calculators, or cellular phones are easily dropped or misplaced. Such equipment is often expensive, but that isn't the only reason to treat it with care. Items that are well cared for last longer than things that are abused.

Borrowing or lending. The portability of much electronic equipment makes lending something a possibility that doesn't exist for other items. (When was the last time you asked to borrow a washing machine?) Ask permission before borrowing such items from friends or family. Return the item promptly, with fully charged batteries, and in the same condition as when it was loaned to you. If you should break anything while using it, the responsibility for repair or replacement is yours. Always treat someone else's equipment as you want them to treat yours.

Keep in mind that you don't *have* to lend your possessions if you don't think they will be well cared for. If Joanne asks to borrow your Walkman because she's *lost* the last two she owned, think carefully before agreeing. Any time you choose to lend an item you own, tell the borrower how to use it properly. Discuss what kind of care you expect, and when you want it to back. Politely make it clear that if your equipment is broken, you expect it to be replaced.

Think

Think how you'd feel if someone took something from your room and failed to return it, or left a lot of their stuff in your space. Think how you'd feel if your parents treated you the way you sometimes treat them when you are in a less than good mood.

The Family Car

Use of the family car is probably the biggest privilege and responsibility a teen can have. This privilege indicates your parents' trust in you, but it's a privilege that can be taken away if you do not take the responsibility seriously.

You realize that a car is an expensive possession, costly both to buy and to maintain. Extra insurance fees are charged because of your use of the family car, and there are increased costs for gas and maintenance. It would be considerate to help pay for some of these expenses with your allowance or extra money that you earn. . . or you may want to trade services, such as car washing or waxing or chauffeuring your little brother in exchange for a certain number of gallons of gasoline.

You'll be excited about using the car when you first get your license, but remember that the family car does belong to your parents and they have the first right to it. The following pointers will help keep your parents happy and you driving:

Ask in advance. When you know ahead of time that you'll need to use the car, ask then, so your parents can plan accordingly. Take turns riding with friends so you aren't asking for the car every weekend.

Never take the car without permission. Doing so is the best way we know to betray your parents' trust and lose driving privileges. Just because *you* know you have the family car doesn't mean your parents know it too. They just might report it stolen. Besides, it's important that your parents know where you are going with their car.

Obey the law. We've never met anyone who didn't know someone who had been killed in an automobile accident during their teen years. Speeding, racing, or driving after drinking can kill or injure you or your passengers. The consequences can send you to jail, revoke your license, or change your life forever. It's not worth it. Stay within the speed limit. If you are old enough to drink legally always designate a driver, and never ever allow friends to drive drunk.

Offer to run errands. Doing so before you are asked pays a lot of dividends. You'll pile up lots of credit by taking your little sister to dancing lessons or going—cheerfully—for a forgotten quart of milk.

Clean out the car after using it. Your Mom won't think it's funny if she sits on a half-eaten chocolate bar in her good dress—you won't think it's too funny either!

Accept "no" gracefully. There will be times when it is not possible for you to use the family car. Try to understand the reason permission was denied without stomping your feet or slamming doors. Temper tantrums only make your parents mad, and they rarely get you the results you want.

When Things Go Wrong in Your Family

With You

How do you behave around the house and how much trouble do you cause? Do you smile more than you frown? Are you a good listener? Do you share both your joys and your sorrows with your family? Do you treat other members of the family as you would wish to be treated?

How do you act at home when you are depressed or upset about something? Do you yell at your brothers and sisters for no apparent reason? Do you turn the radio up full blast to drown out your troubles? Do you slam doors and stomp your feet? Do you close yourself in your room, coming out only for meals and phone calls? Do you give your parents the old silent treatment?

If so, it's no wonder that your family is impatient with you and makes your life more miserable than it already is. How can they help you or support you if you won't share what's on your mind? There is nothing so awful that it can't be shared with those who love and care about you. The risk is well worth the reward. The next time you feel bad, say it out loud and see what happens.

With Your Family

The two biggest causes of stress for people of any age are change and loss. As a teenager, you are "losing" your childhood and "changing" into an adult, and your parents are "losing" a child. So even if you don't have any of the big problems mentioned below, you'll have a certain amount of stress that comes from just growing up!

Sometimes there is trouble in your family that is not your fault. Perhaps your parents are fighting, or considering separation and divorce. Maybe they are

HOW YOU CAN HELP IN TROUBLED TIMES

Be understanding. Realize that every family has problems of one kind or another. Put yourself in other family members' shoes and try to imagine what you would do. Ask questions. Offer to help.

Respect confidences. When someone in your family confides in you, they do so because they trust you. Do everything in your power to respect that trust.

Remain neutral. You don't have to take sides. Fights between your parents usually have nothing to do with you. Of course they make you uncomfortable, but you can feel better by taking a walk, playing your radio with earphones, or calling a friend. When the fight is over, talk to your parents as calmly as you can about how their fighting made you feel: "When you and Dad fight, I get scared that you are going to get a divorce."

Realize you aren't trapped. Use friends, school, sports, volunteer work, odd jobs, and extracurricular activities to make up for some of the fun and happiness that are missing from home during troubled times.

divorced, and you have to adjust to living with just one parent or dividing your time between the two. Perhaps one of your parents has remarried and you have to live with and get to know a stepparent, stepbrothers, and stepsisters. That's not easy.

Maybe someone in your family is abusing drugs or alcohol, or is being physically or sexually abused. Perhaps your parent has lost a job or gotten one in a new city, and you have to move. Maybe a family member is ill or has recently died. While you have no control over these circumstances, they directly affect your life and your relationship with other members of your family. Nobody ever said life was fair.

Hints for Coping with Difficult Situations

It's always best if you can turn to your family for help when you have a problem—but it's not always possible. There are some important things you should know about some problems at home.

Divorce

A divorce is the dissolution of a marriage between husband and wife. Your parents are divorcing each other. They are not divorcing you. You have a right to know where and with whom you will live, as well as who will take care of your schooling. Ask your parents these questions at a time when they seem to be quiet and calm. If that time never seems to come, tell them you need to talk with them about your concerns about the divorce. Ask them when a good time would be for everyone to discuss the divorce. If your parents seem unable to discuss the situation together, start with the parent you find it easiest to talk to.

Dating

Most of us don't even think about our parents as people who go on dates. It's weird to watch your Mom or Dad dating someone else when you want them to be together. It may also be lonely for you when one of them finds a new love. Try to talk to your parent about how a new relationship in their life affects you. Remember, though, that dating is difficult at any age (don't you have a little trouble sometimes?). Try to be courteous to, and open-minded about, your parent's date, and sympathetic to your parent's situation. In other words, treat their dates like you'd want them to treat one of yours!

Stepparents and Stepfamilies

A new stepparent or stepsibling probably feels just as awkward toward you as you do toward them. You may still feel some anger about the breakup of your original family. You don't have to choose between your stepparent and your natural parent. You just have to do your best to get along. Try to keep an open mind.

Alcohol and Drug Abuse

Many teens have someone in their family who abuses alcohol or drugs. If you do, the chances that you will also become addicted are greater. If you or a family member has a problem with alcohol or drugs, treatment is free and available. Alcoholics Anonymous will help the user who is willing to admit he or she has a problem, and they will provide useful information to the user or a family member. Al-Anon is a support group for family members, even if the user is not in treatment. Similar support is available from a variety of programs modeled on the techniques most widely associated with AA. No matter what substance is being abused, help is available.

Even if the abuser refuses to participate, you can learn many useful techniques to help you cope with the situation. And there is no charge for most of these services. Toll-free hot lines that can direct you to groups in your area are easily found in your phone book. These groups keep information confidential and they can be extremely helpful.

Physical and Sexual Abuse

If you or one of your brothers or sisters is being physically or sexually abused by one of your parents, you will have to ask another adult for help. No doubt the abuser is telling you to keep what he or she is doing to you a secret. Don't. Speak to your other parent, a trusted relative or teacher, or the school guidance counselor about it. As difficult as it may seem, don't stop until you find an adult who takes you seriously. It is not your fault if you are being abused. You did nothing to encourage it. You are not a bad person. You have the right to say no to anyone who wants to touch any part of your body in a way that makes you uncomfortable. If they do it anyway, tell an adult whom you trust.

Death or Suicide

Most people feel angry when someone they love dies. You think, "How could Dad leave me? I needed him." Or you feel guilty and think, "Maybe if I had been there, it wouldn't have happened." Psychologists have done studies which show that everyone goes through five stages when someone they love dies: shock, denial, anger, guilt, and acceptance. So it's OK—even normal—for you to feel angry and guilty and sad, and you should realize that some of those feelings last for a long time. Share your feelings with family members; they're probably having the same thoughts and they, too, need to talk about them.

More information on all these subjects is available in your school or public library. Don't be embarrassed to check out a book about divorce or abuse or anything else you are worried about. The librarian usually isn't paying attention, but you can always say you're writing a report on the subject if it will make you feel better.

CALLING FOR HELP

Sometimes when you feel you must talk to someone but have no one to turn to, the phone can be a real friend. Call the information operator (411, in most areas) and ask if there is a crisis line in your town. They are ready to help you with any kind of problem. While there is no need for you to be embarrassed, that doesn't mean you won't feel that way when you first call. Try not to let your embarrassment keep you from calling. You'll find a caring and understanding person on the other end of the line who won't ask for your last name or tell anyone about the call.

If you have a specific problem to talk about, your phone book has listings in the business pages for toll-free information about Alcoholics Anonymous, Al-Anon, abortion counseling, AIDS, pregnancy, rape, sexual abuse, and crisis counseling. You may get additional toll-free numbers by calling 1-800-555-1212 (the toll-free information number in the United States), or by using the toll-free directory at your public or school library.

If you're more comfortable with the computer, you may be able to find on-line help through a news-group or use group dealing with problems similar to yours. When joining a new group it's a good idea to "lurk" for a while to observe the group's interaction.

Be aware that those offering you help or advice via computer may not be qualified to do so—and may even steer you wrong or take advantage of your vulnerability. Don't respond immediately;

CALLING FOR HELP
(Continued)

take time to think; don't answer any questions that make you uncomfortable; and certainly don't set up a private meeting or give your address or phone number to someone who may turn out to be untrustworthy.

Long-term help is best obtained from a qualified professional or reputable group.

Just remember that help is available—all you have to do is reach out for it.

2

COMMUNICATION

Communicating Without Words: Your Appearance

When It Matters

You never get a second chance at a first impression, and a first impression is often based on how you look. Therefore, make the most of what you have. Being well groomed, attractively and appropriately dressed can influence friends at school, keep your parents from nagging you about how you look, make an impression at a job interview, and grab the attention of that special person you want to impress.

When It Doesn't

There is hardly a time when your appearance does-n't matter. It's a matter of courtesy to others to be pleasant to look at. When you're lounging around the house by yourself, though, or just hanging out with family and close friends, it's OK to slob out a little. Be careful not to take your family or your steady for granted, though. They deserve to see you at your best every now and then.

What's Appropriate

The perfect outfit for a rock concert is not necessar-ily the perfect outfit for church with your parents. One of the biggest mistakes teens make where their appearance is concerned is failing to dress appropri-ately. Most of the fights you have with adults over what you wear probably have to do with appropri-ateness. Such disagreements can often be resolved by letting you pick what you wear when you're with your friends, and letting an adult you trust approve what you wear when you're with adults.

Naturally, your clothing is an expression of who you are and, no doubt, you are developing your per-sonal style. Nevertheless, there will be times when what you "feel" like wearing is inappropriate. A baseball cap and a flannel shirt tied around your waist is not acceptable at your great aunt's funeral—even if she did once tell you she admired your style. Take the time to dress properly (if you're not sure, ask); it may make the difference in whether or not you get that job or scholarship.

First Words: Meeting and Greeting

People notice how you look when they first meet you but they also notice what you say and how you act. So, what is the best way to meet or introduce someone. . . and what do you say?

Meeting

Everyone has trouble with introductions. How many times have you walked up to a group of people, hoping to be introduced, and been ignored instead? Have you ever forgotten your best friend's name when the time came to introduce him or her? We've all had such awkward moments, but since we know how it feels, all the more reason to try harder. Maybe these hints will help.

When you are introduced for the first time: Stand (if you aren't already), smile, look the person in the eyes, extend your right hand and give a firm handshake. Listen very carefully for the person's name while saying, "Hi, I'm Joe Friendly." Repeating your name helps the person you've just met remember it, and it also rescues the person introducing you, who may have momentarily blanked on your last name.

When introducing yourself to someone, just smile, shake his hand, and say, "Hi! My name is Cathy Cordial." If he doesn't respond by telling you his name, you may say, "What's your name?" It's never inappropriate to introduce yourself to someone and it's a great way to meet people at a party, at church, or at school. Use this technique, too, when you approach a group and no one introduces you.

When introducing people to one another, always give first and last names, if you can remember them.

When introducing someone to a group, you can introduce them to everyone in the group—"Joe Friendly, this is Justin Jock, Sally Smiley, and Mary Maker"—or, if the group is large, you can say something like, "Listen, everybody, I want you to meet my friend Joe Friendly, who is visiting from Canada. Please introduce yourselves."

When you've forgotten a name, it's not the end of the world. When reintroducing yourself, you can be direct and say, "I'm sorry. I know we've met, but I don't remember your name. I'm Joe Friendly." When introducing someone you know to someone whose name you don't remember, you simply look at the person whose name you don't remember and say, "Do you know my friend Cathy Cordial?" You then pause and hope he'll reply with his own name. If he doesn't, you just keep on talking and Cathy may never find out his name. The other really up-front and honest approach (one we use often) is to say when introducing two people, "I'm sorry. I forget my own mother's name under pressure. Would you please introduce yourselves?"

It's important to note that all of these solutions are less awkward than not introducing someone at all.

Making Conversation

One of the hardest parts of meeting a new person is making conversation with them. Unless the person introducing you has given you a conversation starter—such as, "Freddie just moved here from Kalamazoo"—you may not know where to begin. Try these conversation starters:

Ask a question that does not have a yes or no answer—something like, "How do you know Cathy?" (the person who introduced you) or "Tell me a little about yourself." Ask, "Tell me about your plans for the summer" instead of "Do you have any plans for the summer?"

Listen to what the other person has to say. Being a good listener is part of being a good talker. Follow up on the conversation starter with something like, "Tell me about Kalamazoo. I've heard a lot about it, but I've never been there." Listen to the response and go from there.

At a party, you might start a cold conversation with something like, "What do you think about this music?" If the response is, "I think it's great. I've been following this band for years," you might talk about that. If the response is, "I don't think much about music, it doesn't matter to me," then you would obviously introduce another subject—"What *do* you like?"

Avoid offensive subjects. Ethnic jokes, slurs, even seemingly innocent comments can inadvertently get a conversation off on the wrong foot. Talking about a "hot" political issue or even a contested sports event can lead to a heated conversation with someone you don't know well—not always the best way to start a friendship. Save those spicy conversations until you know one another better.

Avoid gossip. Although it may seem a great way to fill the gap in a conversation, don't do it. Think how you feel when you learn someone has been talking about you behind your back. Also, a comment like "Did you hear about Jeff and Donna?" will be really embarrassing if the response is, "No, Donna is my sister. Tell me what you heard."

Choose your listener carefully. Sharing your

feelings with friends and family can lead to deeper, more meaningful relationships. However, it is important to know who you can trust with your feelings. You've probably experienced a time when you shared a thought or feeling with a "friend" who then embarrassed you by repeating it. If you pay attention, you will know whom to trust with your friendship and feelings.

Use thoughtful words.

"Please," when you're asking for something.

"Thank you," when you get it.

"Excuse me," when you've interrupted someone, or when you want to leave the table.

"I'm sorry," when you've offended.

"No," when you're asked to do something that you know is wrong or that you really don't want to do. Yes, "No" really can be a thoughtful word. It's much better to refuse to do something you really don't want to do than to agree to it and fail to follow through.

Listen to yourself. Do you whine? Do you use the same words over and over? Do you use too many "cuss" words? Do you grunt instead of saying yes or no? There are times when a certain way of speaking, like a certain style of clothing, is appropriate, and times when it isn't. Make a conscious choice to speak appropriately.

KNOW WHEN TO SPEAK UP AND WHEN TO BE QUIET

It's OK. . .
to speak to a fellow passenger on a plane, train, bus, or automobile, if they want to talk.

It's not OK. . .
to initiate a conversation if your fellow passenger is reading or sleeping.

It's OK. . .
to smile at a passing stranger on the street.

It's not OK. . .
to go anywhere alone with a stranger or someone you've just met.

It's OK. . .
to talk to your dance partner while dancing, if you want to.

It's not OK. . .
to talk to a friend who is working if, by talking to you, he is not doing his job.

It's OK. . .
to talk to someone you don't know at school, church, or a party.

It's not OK. . .
to go somewhere alone with that someone until you know them better.

It's OK. . .
to say what's on your mind in a constructive way (see "Talk About It," in Chapter 1).

KNOW WHEN TO SPEAK UP AND WHEN TO BE QUIET
(Continued)

It's not OK. . .
to "sass" an adult, teacher, or friend, or to disrupt a class or conversation with inappropriate comments.

In summary, *think before you speak!* (This goes for phone conversations, too.)

Telephone Communication

You'll probably never again spend as much time on the phone as you do now. If you're fortunate enough to have your own phone line, then you won't have some of the problems of those who must share their time with the other people in the house. In either case, learning to be courteous and considerate on the phone is a skill that will always serve you well—both in your personal life and in your future occupation.

Making Calls

Identify Yourself
Don't you hate it when you're in the middle of doing something and someone calls and launches into a

long conversation and you have no earthly idea who they are? Or worse, when you answer the phone and someone says, "Guess who this is?" It's hard to identify your own sister's voice sometimes if she calls when you're thinking about something else. Don't put anyone in a position you wouldn't want to be in yourself. To be on the safe side *always* identify yourself.

A BRIEF WORD ABOUT GIRLS CALLING BOYS

Though many of your parents will have trouble with this, it's OK for girls to call boys. As a matter of fact, many boys like it. What they don't like, though, is a girl who persists in calling often, even though he's tried to make it clear he's not interested. (Note: Girls don't like this behavior in boys, either.)

Check Your Timing

Try not to call one person's house too often. Though you might think you have to communicate your thoughts with your best friend the minute you think them, it's better to save up a few thoughts and make fewer phone calls. Why? Because even though your friend loves to talk to you, your friend's family may be annoyed with all your phone calls. You'll make a better impression on them if you call less. And remember what time it is when you call. Unless you absolutely, positively know its OK to call at any hour, limit your calls to between 8 A.M. and 10 P.M.

Check Convenience

Ask if it's a good time to talk when you call someone just to chat. You may know that the best time to reach a friend at home is during dinner or a favorite television show, and although your friend may talk with you, he or she might rather do so at a different time. Ask. Then when you do talk, you'll have someone who really wants to listen on the other end of the line.

When You Call a Wrong Number

apologize to the person you've disturbed, but check the number with him so you'll know whether you misdialed or copied the number incorrectly.

A WORD ABOUT CAR PHONES

A car phone should be used with discretion. Talk time is much more expensive on a car phone than a pay phone or your home phone. Therefore, long conversations with your friends are inappropriate. Because your attention may be diverted from your driving, they can also be dangerous. Remember, too, that it feels awkward for a passenger in your car to be sitting there while you have a long conversation with someone else on the car phone. Save those calls for later, and spend your talk time with your passenger.

Taking Calls

Try to Sound Interested in What the Caller has to Say

Obviously he or she thought it was important enough to share with you. If you're really distracted and having trouble paying attention, ask if you can return the call later.

Excuse Yourself Before Talking to Someone Else in the Room

Don't you feel silly when the person you're talking to on the phone starts talking to someone else in the room, but you think he's talking to you, so you start trying to figure out what he's talking about, and then you realize he's not talking to you? Don't you wish he'd just said, "Hang on a minute, Jeff" so that you'd know what he said next was not intended for you? The least you can do for someone on the phone before talking to someone in the room is to say, "Hold on a minute."

Make Sure You Are Not Disturbing Others

Take calls in a different room if your talking on the phone would disturb someone else who is trying to watch TV, read, sleep, do their homework, or anything else that doesn't involve you.

Try Not to Eat Noisily While You're Talking on the Phone

It sounds weird on the other end of the line, and it

feels kind of like being in a room with somebody who's having a snack but doesn't offer you any.

When the Call is for Someone Else

When the call is for someone else, especially an adult, get the name of the caller, put down the phone gently, and go tell them they have a call. Don't yell. This may not seem like a big deal to you, but it makes a difference to adults.

Take Good Messages

Ask the caller to spell his name and give you the number where he can be reached. Repeat it back to make sure you have the information correct. Write down the time you took the message and place it in a prominent place—where you know the person it is intended for will see it. Most households find it useful to have a central message area, a place that everyone knows to check for notes or phone messages.

Using Someone Else's Phone

At a place of business, use the phone only if it relates to that business or there is no pay phone nearby. Perhaps you need to cancel a lunch date or let someone know you're running late. Keep the call brief. Never use a business phone just to pass the time.

While you're working, use the phone only for work-related calls. You're being paid to do a job, and you can't do it if you're visiting on the phone with a friend.

To make a long-distance call from a phone other than your own, you must have a good reason, and you should ask the permission of the person to whom the phone belongs. Offer to reimburse them for the cost of the call unless you have a calling card, can call collect, or can charge the call to your own number.

To use someone else's car or cellular phone, you must also ask permission. Ask only if the call is an important one; keep the call brief, and offer to reimburse for the cost of the call.

Telephone Dos and Don'ts

For safety's sake. . .

Do tape police, fire, ambulance, and local poison-control center numbers on the phone. (Tape your address to the phone, while you're at it. In an emergency even the simplest details can be hard to remember.) Trying to look up the number for the fire department when the ceiling is about to cave in is dangerous. If you suspect fire, get out of the building first, then go next door to call. If you think you hear an intruder, lock yourself in a room with a telephone, call the police, and stay there until they arrive. And if it makes you feel safer, stay on the line with the emergency operator until the police get to your home.

Do, if you have a home burglar alarm connected to a central monitoring station, know how to contact the station in case of a false alarm or a real need.

Do hang up on anyone who says something scary or obscene, or something you don't understand. *Do not* talk with them or answer any questions. Tell an adult immediately about the call. If obscene calls continue, let the phone company know and follow their recommendations. Your phone book contains guidelines for handling such calls.

For courtesy's sake. . .

Do keep a list of frequently called numbers near the phone, or if your phone has a "quick dial" feature, let it remember for you. Guessing a number or calling from memory and getting the wrong number takes longer than looking up the number on your "quick list."

Do have a central message area, someplace where everyone knows to check for notes or phone messages. Just put the message there as soon as you take it and you don't have to remember to tell anyone later. It is each family member's responsibility to check the message area when they've been away from home.

Do negotiate call times with your family or ask their permission if you think you'll be on the phone for a while. Making an effort to accommodate your family's needs encourages them to make an effort to accommodate yours.

Don't place a call before 8 a.m. or after 10 p.m. Even if you know your friend stays up until midnight, your call can disturb his family. Adults usually prefer quiet after 10!

Don't you, or a friend, make any call from your home phone, cellular phone, car phone, fax, or modem that incurs extra charges. Unless you pay the bill, you must ask the permission of the person who does.

Don't call 900 numbers without an adult's permission. They are very costly, and you'll get caught when the phone bill arrives anyway.

Phone Gadgets

Call Waiting

This is a great feature, but it can sometimes prove to be an annoyance. If call waiting is signaling when you're in the middle of a phone call, excuse yourself from the first caller, tell the second caller you'll call back, and go back to the first caller immediately. Make yourself a note so you won't forget to call the second person.

Answering Machines

◆ Do not leave your answering machine on unless you intend to return the calls.

◆ Return calls within 48 hours, unless you are out of town.

◆ Make sure your incoming and outgoing messages are not offensive. We've heard quite a few that were humorous, but terribly inappropriate. Think about *everyone* who may hear your message before you record it.

◆ If you share an answering machine with adults in your house who may be receiving business calls, let them record the message. An appropriate one would be, "This is the Jones residence. We're sorry we're unable to take your call right now, but if you'll leave your name, number, and a brief message at the sound of the tone, we'll get back to you just as soon as possible." We prefer "You have reached the Jones residence" to "You have reached 123-4567," because the latter doesn't help someone who may have reached a wrong number. However, some people prefer not to announce their name, and if that is the case it's all right to give the number instead.

◆ If a message is left on your machine that is obviously for someone else, it is polite to inform the caller that they reached a wrong number.

Caller ID

If you are living away from your parents, perhaps

sharing an off-campus apartment, you may want to install one of these machines, but unless you are having a problem with harassing phone calls, we really don't see the need for a Caller ID machine. If you wish to screen your calls, an answering machine can serve many of the same functions. Of course, Caller ID lets you know everyone who called, whether they left a message or not. It seems to us like an expensive gadget that keeps you from learning how to handle phone calls appropriately—even the ones you don't want.

Calling Cards

A "calling card" or telephone credit card may allow you to make calls to or from your home more conveniently. It can also be used to make calls from a pay phone when you have no change. These cards can be very helpful if you travel—perhaps between relatives' homes or to summer camp, or to college away from home. You and your family will have to decide who pays for what, but such cards are certainly a convenient way to stay in touch.

Beepers

Some teens wear a beeper so that working parents or an invalid relative is able to get in touch at all times. If your family suggests it and one of you is willing to pay the charges, go for it. If you are beeped in the presence of others, turn off the noise, excuse yourself, and return the call promptly. There is no need to explain the call when you return to the group unless you must leave. Then a simple, "I'm sorry, my mother is ill," should suffice.

Realize, though, that some teens wearing beepers are involved in criminal activities such as drug deals. In some areas, you may be questioned by law-enforcement officials just for wearing one.

Electronic Correspondence

At one time all social correspondence was handwritten, on lovely monogrammed stationery. It wasn't even acceptable to type something unless you were physically disabled. Boy, have times changed. Facsimile (fax) and electronic mail (e-mail) seem to be the preferred method of correspondence for your generation. Although they can be quick and easy, lack of privacy and expense can be a deterrent to their use. Here are a few tips.

Fax

The advantage to fax communication is that it is fast, and sometimes less expensive than a lengthy telephone conversation. It can be a great way for friends and family who are separated to stay in touch.

Remember, though, that unless someone has a private fax machine at home, the equipment is usually located at an office or mailing center. What you write can be read by anyone who walks by the machine. A fax may be marked confidential, but unless you are standing there as it is received, there is nothing confidential about the process. Most especially with electronic correspondence, you must be cautious about what you write. And, as with any letter, use proper form and punctuation.

E-mail

On-line "use groups" and electronic bulletin boards have opened new avenues of meeting and communicating with people who have similar interests. E-mail also allows almost instant communication with friends and relatives who have access to the system. It provides a great way to keep in touch or make new friends.

E-mail is not necessarily confidential or private, and some adults have used the system to seduce or entice young people into illegal activities. Be aware that the new friend you meet in a use group may be sincere, but he may also be masquerading as something he is not. Therefore, you should be cautious about any personal contact you make with someone you "meet" on-line.

Just as you may be uncomfortable discussing certain topics in face-to-face conversations, you may choose not to respond, or to change the subject, of any electronic chat in which questions are asked that you don't wish to answer. Also, you should not include any subject matter in an E-mail transmission that you would not be comfortable having anyone else see.

Check and respond to your E-mail messages promptly. However, if you are a student who uses your computer for papers and homework and are often interrupted with E-mail transmissions, perhaps it would be a good idea to set up a time when you'd prefer to receive transmissions from friends— then you won't be tempted to stop studying to converse.

Of course there will be typos and errors made in the course of communicating via E-mail. Your communication can be easier to understand, though, if you use proper form, spelling, and grammar.

Although the charge can be less than a phone call of the same length, electronic correspondence is not free. Charges depend on the type of communication you choose. Know what those charges are and be sure that you (or whoever is paying) can afford them.

Personal Correspondence

Even if you spend all of your time surfing the Internet and chatting electronically with people across the country and around the world, there are times when it is preferable to handwrite personal correspondence. Thank-you or sympathy notes should be written on personalized notepaper, if you have it, and sent by snail mail. There are a few guidelines you need to know, if you've never done this before.

Pen and Paper

Choose a paper that is appropriate for your corre-spondence. Personal letters to close friends and family can be written on decorative, colorful, or "fun" paper using ink of any color. Business letters, which may be written to inquire about a job or to purchase or return merchandise, should be written on paper of conservative color (which means white, cream, or light gray) with minimal decoration, and if not typed, should be written in black ink. For long letters, use letter-size stationery with second sheets. For short correspondence, use a card or fold-over note.

As a teen, you must write with a pen rather than a pencil. If you have trouble writing without making too many mistakes (lots of people do), draft what you want to say before using your good paper.

Personal letters should be neatly handwritten, unless your handwriting is too hard to read. It's preferable to type business letters, but whether the letter is typewritten or not, always sign your full name by hand, with your name typed below your signature.

Form

Once the pen and paper are ready, write the date at the upper right side of the page. On personal let-ters, all you need to write is "Wednesday" or

"September 1." On business letters, write the complete date—month, date, and year.

It's not necessary to write out your address if you're using a plain sheet of paper. But if you want to, it goes in the upper right-hand corner just above the date. An alternative is to put both the address and date in the lower left corner of the page.

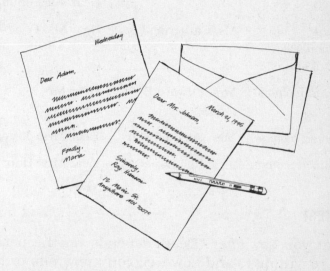

Your letter begins with "Dear___." How it ends depends on who's getting the letter. "Sincerely" is always correct for business letters or letters to mere acquaintances. "Love," "Fondly," or "Affectionately" are correct for friends and relatives. You can also close a letter to a good friend with a phrase such as "Hoping to see you next week," or "Miss you a lot," or just "Always."

Correct forms of address are as follows:

Boys under 7	Master Michael Ruiz	Dear Michael
Boys 7–18	Adam Rabalais	Dear Adam
Man 18 or over	Mr. Peter Myers	Dear Peter or Dear Mr. Myers
Unmarried girl	Miss Emily Phillips	Dear Emily or Dear Miss Phillips
Woman (unknown marital status)	Ms. Catherine Fry	Dear Ms. Fry
Married woman	Mrs. Edward E. Jeffries	Dear Mrs. Jeffries
Divorced woman	Mrs. Jill Johnson	Dear Mrs. Johnson
Widowed woman	Mrs. Roy Hanson	Dear Mrs. Hanson

Content

What you say after "Dear" depends on the person you're writing to and how well you know him or her. The personal letters that are the most fun to read are the ones that sound as if the writer is talking to you. Underline words, capitalize them, use exclamation points, dashes, and contractions. Write personal letters that sound like the way you talk. After you've written the latest news about yourself, ask some questions that your friend can answer when he or she writes back.

Business letters, on the other hand, should get straight to the point and specify what action needs to be taken. For example:

Dear Sunglass Company:

On April 27th, I bought a pair of your "jazz"-style sunglasses. Yesterday, during the course of normal use, I accidentally dropped my glasses and the left lens popped out of the frame. Since the glasses are still under warranty, I would appreciate a speedy repair. I enclose a return-address label, and you may contact me at (901) 876-5432 if I can provide any further information.

Thank you,

Joe Cool

The Envelope

When you've written your message, fold the paper to fit the envelope—usually in thirds for letter-size paper and in half for note or small letter paper. Place the paper in the envelope so that when it is removed and opened, it is right side up for the reader.

Your envelope should have a return address (full name, full street address, city, state, and zip code) in the upper left corner and a stamp in the upper right corner. The mailing address is centered on the face of the envelope, with the second and third lines aligned below the first.

At one time the custom was to indent the second and third lines of the address, but this is rarely done any longer. It is particularly difficult for U.S. Postal Service equipment to scan addresses that are not aligned.

Greeting Cards

There are greeting cards to say almost anything, and they can be very good for expressing something that is difficult to say. From alcoholism to AIDS, from birthdays to bar mitzvahs, the right card is available for every occasion if you look hard enough. Be sure, though, to add just a few personal lines to a preprinted card. It lets the reader know you chose the card especially for him or her.

Invitations

A good invitation can really get a guest excited about attending a party. In addition to giving the pertinent information about time, place, hosts, attire, and occasion, it should also convey the theme and feeling of the event. A good party or stationery store can be helpful in choosing just the right invitation.

Most invitations you receive will be informal; they will be fill-in, preprinted cards or casually worded printed ones. If "RSVP" is followed by a phone number, then you simply call and let the host know whether or not you'll attend. If it's followed by an address, then a short note to the host, such as "Looking forward to your football party Saturday night," is sufficient. If the invitation says "Regrets only," then you need to respond only if you won't attend.

Be sure you respond promptly. Since the host usually has to prepare, or have a caterer prepare, food for a certain number of people several days before the event, calling at the last minute can throw things into a tailspin. The host usually has to pay for the number of guests he anticipated would attend rather than the actual number who do—so be sure you go if you say you're going to, and let the host know well in advance whether or not you'll be attending.

Occasionally you'll receive a formal invitation, one that is engraved or handwritten, in the third person, on white or cream cards. As with informal invitations, your response should "match" the invitation. Your formal response should be written in the third person following the correct form. An invitation to a debutante dance might read:

Mr. and Mrs. Rich Worthington

Miss Vera Worthington

request the pleasure of your company

at The Assembly Ball

on Friday, the fifth of February

at half after seven o'clock

The Tuxedo Club

Tuxedo Park, New York

R.s.v.p.
18 Park Place
New York, New York 10001

Your acceptance would read:

Miss Sue Unworthy

accepts with pleasure

the kind invitation of

Mr. and Mrs. Worthington and

Miss Worthington

for Friday, the fifth of February

at half after seven o'clock

Your regret would follow the same form, substituting "regrets that she is unable to accept" for "accepts with pleasure."

Sometimes an invitation includes a response card, which looks like this:

Warren Harris

☐ accepts
☐ regrets
    Friday, February fifth
    The Tuxedo Club

or

M_____

will ____ attend

Friday, February fifth

All you must do with a response card is fill in your name, indicate whether you accept or regret, and return it as soon as possible.

Thank-You Notes

Much of your personal correspondence is optional. You don't *have* to send a birthday card or a newsy letter to a friend at camp. Thank-you notes, however, are *required* if you have not enthusiastically thanked the giver in person.

Points to Remember for Writing Thank-You Notes:

◆ Write the note promptly after the event or receipt of the gift—preferably within a week, but better late than never!

◆ Make it sound friendly and sincere: "I just love the sweater you sent for my birthday—you must have known blue was my favorite color" is better than "Thank you so much for the blue sweater you sent for my birthday."

◆ Always mention anything that was special about the gift or event: "I loved spending the Easter holidays with you and your family in Florida. I'll never forget flounder fishing by flashlight and our bonfire on the beach."

◆ Never mention anything that was wrong with the gift or event: "How thoughtful of you to make homemade fudge for my birthday. Our whole family enjoyed it" is better than "My family said the homemade fudge you sent for my birthday was delicious. I didn't get to eat any because I'm allergic to chocolate."

◆ When acknowledging a gift of money, give some

idea of what you plan to do with it: "The fifty dollars you sent for Christmas will really help me get the bike I'm saving for" is better than "I put the fifty dollars you gave me in my bank. I know it will come in handy someday."

◆ It's not necessary to write a note for something you have already thanked the giver for enthusiastically in person, but a note is always appreciated. *Exception:* When you have traveled with someone or been their houseguest, you must write a note no matter how profusive your verbal thanks were.

Sympathy Notes

For many people, these are the hardest notes to write. It's important, though, to make the effort because it means so much to the recipient, and because you may feel better for having expressed your grief or sadness. A handwritten note is always preferable to a purchased greeting card, but it need not be long. Try to include an anecdote or something special you remember about the person who died.

Dear Mr. and Mrs. Jackson,

I was so shocked to hear of John's sudden death. We didn't see each other much except during football season, but I'll never forget the time he recovered the ball that I fumbled on the five-yard line. He really saved my skin!

John always kept the team's spirits up when we thought we were losing the game. We'll all miss him.

I know this is a terrible time for you, but please let me know if there is anything I can do.

> Very sincerely,
>
> *Tommy Thomas*

If a close member of your family dies, you may need to help acknowledge flowers, gifts, and written letters of condolence; printed sympathy cards do not require an answer. The funeral home may provide you with printed acknowledgement cards, but they should not be used without the addition of a short handwritten note.

In response to letters written to you, you might say:

Dear Joanne,

Your letter arrived at a time when I really needed the support of my friends. It is a great comfort to know how many people loved Dad, and I want to thank you for writing.

> Much love,
>
> *Linda*

When you're writing the letter for your mother or father (or as a close friend of the family of the deceased) the wording is a little different.

Dear Mrs. Howard,

Mother asked me to write and tell you how grateful she was for your sweet letter. I would like to add my thanks to you for writing. Notes like yours have been such a great help to all of us at this time.

Sincerely,

Marie Faulkner

Journal Keeping

Although keeping a journal is a form of correspondence with oneself rather than with another, it is a very useful form of writing. Many English classes encourage their students to keep journals because the practice teaches an important and personal form of expression. Because your personal journal is for your eyes only, you can say whatever you think or feel, and it's a very good way to work through some difficult issues in your life. Taking the time to write down what you think and feel, then putting it away and going back to it later, can really help you take a look at what's going on in your life and get you through some hard times. We encourage you to try it.

3

MEALTIME MANNERS

When you say the word "etiquette," many people think first of table manners. It's probably the reason many of you own this book—some adult in your life *really* wanted to improve your table manners and give you some idea of how to behave, *or* you've realized there are times when you're uncomfortable with your table manners and you want to improve them.

It's no wonder you're unsure of yourself at times. Think about how you eat most of your meals. Breakfast on the run. . . lunch in a crowded, noisy, school cafeteria, in your favorite fast-food restaurant, or in the car. . . and dinner in front of the TV. None of those require much in the way of service, utensils, or polite conversation.

As with anything else, practicing your dining skills will help you feel more at ease in situations that matter. What, you ask, is a situation that matters?   You'll know it when you're in it—maybe it's dinner with a special date, maybe it's dining with a friend's family, maybe it's eating out in a fancy restaurant for a special occasion. But you need to practice ahead of time so you'll be ready. This is going to require a little effort on your part.

Family Meals at Home

With more parents working and more teens spending time at home alone, perhaps more of the responsibility for meals has fallen to you. Even it it hasn't, pitching in at family meals is a wonderful way for you to help out and learn some dining skills.

Family style at your house may be eating a pizza from the box or munching a sandwich in front of the TV. We all eat like that occasionally, maybe often, but it is important to realize that we don't have to. Just because you're dining alone on a bowl of soup and a sandwich, you don't have to slob out! You can put a placemat, napkin, and spoon on the table, turn on your favorite music, take a good book or magazine to the table, and have a leisurely dinner enjoying your own company and the meal you prepared. Who cares if your brother and sister call you a snob while they chow down standing at the kitchen counter?

Good table manners should be learned and practiced at home. You may not think so now, but some day when you are president of the company, you'll be glad you learned to set the table, sit up straight, and use your napkin properly.

Setting the Table

Try to set the table for the whole family at least once a week. It helps you learn where the forks, knives, spoons, plates, glasses, and napkins go. It's also important for your family to be together at mealtime; sometimes it's the only chance during the day you all have to be with and talk to one another.

When you set the table you need only put out the utensils to be used for that meal. If you're having sandwiches and chips, you don't need any flatware—just a plate, napkin, and beverage glass. If you're having soup and crackers, all you need is a spoon, soup bowl, plate (if you wish), napkin, and beverage glass. If you're having roast beef, mashed potatoes, and ice cream, then you'll need a plate, fork, knife, spoon, napkin, and beverage glass (and, later, a bowl for the dessert). No one wants to wash any more dishes than they have to!

What Goes Where?

The easy rule about what silverware gets used when is "from the outside in." Use the silverware farthest from the plate first, and with each successive course choose the next piece of silverware, again working from the far side of the plate inward.

Forks always go to the left of the plate, with the fork to be used first placed farthest from the plate. Exceptions to this rule are the seafood-cocktail fork and the dessert fork. The fork for a seafood cocktail is placed to the right of the spoons. The dessert fork may be placed closest to the plate on the left or above the dinner plate, or it may be brought in with the dessert.

Knives always go on the right, next to the plate, with the sharp edge of the blade facing in. That will ensure that the letters are showing if the silver is monogrammed.

Spoons always go to the right of the knives. The dessert spoon may also be placed above the plate or brought in with dessert.

A *service plate* is seen more often in restaurants than in private homes. You will know it when you see it because it is larger than a dinner plate and is used under the plates for the appetizer, soup, and salad courses. It is removed when the entree is brought in on the dinner plate.

Glasses are placed a little to the right of the tip of the knife.

The *cup and saucer* are placed to the right of the spoons.

The *salad plate* is placed to the left of the forks *if* the salad is served with the entree and not as a separate course.

The *bread and butter plate* is almost always present at restaurant meals, but at home it is usually used only on formal occasions. It should be placed above and slightly to the left of the forks.

Serving the Food

Plates may be filled before they are placed on the table, or the food may be passed in serving dishes after everyone is seated and, if it is customary in your home, grace has been said. Food should be passed from left to right, with each person taking a portion that he thinks he can finish. If you cannot reach an item, ask the person nearest that item to pass it to you. If it's necessary to pass your plate to the head of the table for a second helping, leave the knife and fork on it, but be sure they are securely placed so they won't fall off.

Leaving the Table

You should not leave the table during a meal unless you are coughing or sneezing uncontrollably or need to blow your nose. Try to use the bathroom before you sit at the table, or wait until you are through eating. If you must answer the phone during a meal, tell the caller you are eating and ask to call him or her back when you are finished.

When Everyone has Eaten

When everyone is finished, napkins should be neatly placed on the table—unfolded to the side of the plate, *not* crumpled up on it. It's also nice if each person takes his plate to the kitchen. If you *must* leave the table before others are finished, ask to be excused. Do this only when you are pressed for time—not just to go watch your favorite TV program.

Be sure to thank the cook!

Buffet Meals

Buffet meals are definitely the easiest to serve. In the simplest form of buffet, family members serve themselves from the pots in the kitchen and take their food to the table.

A restaurant buffet is also pretty easy to navigate. Usually you serve yourself soup or salad, then go back to the buffet table for your entree, returning again for dessert. As a rule, the waiter brings your beverage and removes dirty dishes. If you go back for seconds do *not* take your used plate with you, but take a clean plate at the buffet.

Buffet meals in your home or someone else's for a special occasion or holiday celebration can take two forms:

1. The hostess places the beverage, flatware, plates, napkins, and food on one or two buffet tables. Guests help themselves and find a place

to sit and eat—not necessarily at a table! Obviously, this is the easiest method for the hostess, and it works well for big gatherings with casual food. It can be lots of fun if the menu is practical and easy to eat while sitting on the floor, the stairs, the sofa, or the piano bench! If no one takes your plate when you are finished, you should take it to the kitchen.

2. The hostess sets the dining table and per-haps some additional tables with silverware, napkins, place cards (if she wishes), and glasses—everything except the dinner plate and the food. Food is placed on a buffet table or side-board. Guests serve themselves and put their plates at the place assigned by the hostess. When there are no place cards to indicate assigned seats at the table, the guests should place themselves boy, girl, boy, girl and leave the ends of the table for the host and hostess.

Guests should stand behind their chairs until the hostess is seated or asks them to seat themselves. Girls are then seated by the boy on their left. If a girl doesn't have a boy on her left, she should seat herself. (Remember, girls, if given the opportunity, stand to the right of that boy you've had a crush on for weeks!)

This type of service is the most difficult for the hostess because it requires more advance preparation, but it is the easiest for the guest—no worrying about where to sit, or trying to bal-ance food, beverage, napkin, knife, and fork!

Detailed Table Service and Place Settings

To help you better understand place settings and table service, and to be prepared for any dining situation, let's have an imaginary five-course meal.

The Appetizer

Restaurant menus often begin with a section labeled "appetizers." These are items like shrimp cocktail, oysters, pate, or fruit cocktail. If you order one, the waiter brings the utensil with which to eat it. If you are served an appetizer at a dinner party, use the outermost utensil that looks correct, or watch the hostess and follow her lead. For the shrimp cocktail, you use the cocktail fork. If you were having fruit cocktail, there would be a teaspoon in place of the cocktail fork. If the appetizer you choose requires a fork larger than a cocktail fork, it will be the fork farthest to the left on the outside of your place setting.

Bread and Butter

In restaurants, the bread and butter are often brought before any of the other food. At a private dinner party, the bread may be served with appetizer, soup, or entree.

The small plate just above the forks is the bread and butter plate. When the bread basket is passed, take a piece of bread and place it on your bread and butter plate. Butter should be taken from the butter dish and placed on your bread and butter plate also. (Note: If there is no bread and butter plate, place your slice of bread and pat of butter on the edge of your dinner plate.)

To butter your bread, break off a small piece, hold it close to the plate between your fingers, and spread the butter with your butter knife. Do *not* spread the bread open, hold it flat in the palm of your hand, and slather on butter as if you were making a peanut butter sandwich! When you've eaten the piece of bread you've prepared, repeat the procedure with another.

If you have a bread and butter plate but no small knife, use your dinner knife, propping the tip of it on the top right edge of the bread and butter plate between uses.

The Soup

Once you know that the utensil required to eat the next course will be on the outside, you must choose between the soup spoon and the salad fork. Obviously you choose the soup spoon when soup is served.

If croutons (tiny fried cubes of bread) or oyster crackers are passed, you may sprinkle them directly in your soup. Place larger soda crackers on your bread and butter plate, then break them, a few pieces at a time, into your soup.

The soup course is often the hardest to eat quietly and neatly. It can be done, though, if you hold your spoon properly—the same way you hold your fork: resting on the middle finger of your hand with your thumb on top. Never, never hold it the way you hold your toothbrush!

Tilt and move the spoon away from you to fill it with soup. Then lift the spoon to your mouth as you lean from the waist over the bowl. Never hunch over the bowl and lower your mouth to the soup! When the soup reaches your lips, quietly sip it from the side or end of the spoon. It is not necessary, or proper, to put the entire spoon into your mouth, unless you're eating a chunky soup that can't be sipped.

If the soup is served in a soup cup or a cream-soup bowl with handles, it is permissible to pick up the cup and drink the soup from it; but you may also use a spoon.

To get that last tasty drop, you must tilt the bowl slightly away from you and, moving the spoon away from you, scoop it up. Scooping the soup and tilting the bowl away from you prevents getting soup in the lap!

When you are between sips of soup (this is called resting), you may leave your spoon in the bowl, if it is a large one, or you may rest it on the saucer underneath. If your soup is served in a small cup or bowl, you should rest the spoon on the saucer between sips. When you are finished, leave the spoon in a large bowl or soup plate, or on the saucer beneath a soup cup or small bowl.

You know, of course, not to blow on your soup. If it's too hot to eat, you may *gently* move your spoon back and forth in the soup to incorporate some air into it and cool it. It's also OK to scoop some soup into your spoon and hold it just over the soup bowl for a moment, while you're talking. If the soup is just *too* hot you may spoon a little ice from your ice water into it. Unfortunately, none of these methods ever seems to work fast enough, but they are the only ones that are acceptable. Spitting hot soup back into the bowl is *never* an option!

The Salad

In America, the salad is usually served with, or just before, the main course. In Europe and many other parts of the world, it is served following the main course. Either way is correct, and if your hostess has set the table properly, you can tell by the placement of the salad fork when the salad will be served. In the illustration above, a salad knife and fork have been provided, and it is clear from the placement of the utensils that the salad is going to be served before the entree.

When the salad is served *with* the entree, there is no need for a salad fork; use the dinner fork. When the salad is served separately from the main course, use the salad fork and salad knife, if one is provided. It is perfectly all right to cut large pieces of lettuce or vegetables with the edge of your salad fork or with the salad fork and knife. However, you should cut only one piece at a time. Don't make a lovely garden salad look like cole slaw by cutting the entire thing into tiny pieces before you eat the first bite!

If you do use a salad knife (or your dinner knife if a salad knife is not provided), it should rest at the top of the plate, blade facing you, when not in use. When you have finished your salad, both the salad fork and knife should be placed in the five o'clock position, as shown in the illustration.

The Main Course or Entree

This is the part of the meal you are most familiar with, and if you look at the illustration you can see that the large knife and fork are the utensils to use for the main course.

Many teens have difficulty with the proper way to hold a knife and fork when cutting and eating. We have seen some very unusual and awkward configurations. Let us explain so you'll always do it right: When you are cutting (no more than a few bites at a time, please), the fork should be in your left hand, tines down, handle cupped in the palm of your hand and pointer finger on the back of the handle pointing toward the tines. The knife should be held in your right hand as illustrated.

To cut, pierce your next bite with the fork, then cut with the knife about one-quarter inch from your fork. If you cut too far away from the fork, the whole piece of meat moves back and forth and may knock other food off your plate. If you cut too big a bite, don't try to put it in your mouth; cut it in half and eat each piece separately.

Once you have the bite on your fork, you may raise it to your mouth, still with the fork tines down, and eat it. This is the Continental or European method. It may look awkward to you, but it is perfectly permissible. More commonly, after cutting the meat, the knife is placed at the top of the plate, blade facing toward the center of the plate. The fork is then transferred to the right hand, tines up, and this long-awaited bite is eaten!

Obviously, any vegetables that are served with the entree are eaten with your fork. Should you need help getting them onto the fork, you may hold a piece of bread, or your knife, down on the plate with your left hand. Hold your left hand in place while you push the fork and vegetable toward it. When they meet, the vegetable will be "pushed" onto your fork.

When you have eaten all you care to, place the knife and fork in the five o'clock position as you did when you finished your salad. (The reason for the five o'clock position is that the server will remove your plate from the right. If your utensils are in that position, he simply clamps his thumb over the handles and carries your plate away.)

If you are left-handed, cutting meat or buttering bread may be a little more difficult. If you've learned to do these things as right-handers do, that's great! But if it feels unnatural to you, then go ahead and hold the knife in your left hand and fork in your right when cutting, and use your left hand to hold your fork when eating. But please do not reverse the place setting itself or the finished position. They should remain as shown.

The Dessert

When preparing to eat dessert, unlike soup or salad, you do not know what utensil to use until you see the food. Relax. The dessert service should be placed on the table above the dinner plate or brought in with the dessert. It is seldom placed to the left or right of the dinner plate (although a dessert spoon may be placed beside the knife). So don't worry if you run out of flatware before dessert.

Diners often linger at the table after dessert. Leave your napkin on your lap until the hostess places hers on the table. When she does, pick yours up in the center with your left hand and place it to the left of your plate. Never wad your napkin or place it on a dirty plate!

DINING DOS

Do wait until everyone is present before sitting at the table. At home you may sit, but do not begin to eat until everyone is present unless Mom or a hostess says, "Please start, I don't want your meal to get cold." This keeps the family from finishing the meal before the cook gets to the table! It's also nice for the boys to practice seating the girls—when the time comes to do it for your date, you'll feel much more comfortable if you've practiced on your sister.

Do put your napkin in your lap as soon as you are seated. It's the first thing you do, even if you are in a restaurant and haven't ordered yet. If the napkin is small, unfold the whole thing in your lap. Resist the temptation to unfold it by flapping it out to the side of your chair! If the napkin is large, you may leave it folded in half in your lap. You may not tuck the napkin under your chin.

DINING DOS
(Continued)

Do tuck your necktie into your shirt between the second and third buttons to prevent unavoidable spots and splatters on your good tie. Put it back in place when you have finished eating.

Do try a little bit of everything when you serve yourself at a friend's home or family meal, unless you know you are allergic to a certain food.

Do keep dinner conversation pleasant. If someone brings up a topic you find unpleasant, ask if they could talk about it later.

Do take small bites and try to avoid talking with food in your mouth.

Do wait until you have swallowed a bite of food before you take a sip of your beverage. Bread crumbs don't look so appetizing on the rim of the glass—and neither does lipstick, girls, so blot your lips before going out to a dinner party.

Do remember your posture at the table. You probably think we mean "Get your elbows off the table," but there are times when it's OK

DINING DOS
(Continued)

to put your elbows on the table. When you are resting between courses or leaning across the table to talk to someone, nothing is more natural. Lounging and slouching over your food at the table, though, are no-no's. To keep food from falling into your lap or onto your shirt when you eat, pull your chair up close enough to the table, about four inches from the edge. Then, keeping your back straight, lean from the waist over the plate while you eat. Anything that drops will fall back on the plate.

DINING DON'TS

Don't let your eyes get bigger than your stomach when dining out. Order what you think you can eat. If you just can't finish, most places are happy to give you a take-home bag. Don't be embarrassed to ask for one—it's a compliment to the chef.

Don't use serving utensils for yourself. Use the sugar spoon to put the sugar in your tea.

DINING DON'TS
(Continued)

Use *your* iced-tea spoon to stir it. Use the butter server to put a pat of butter on your plate. Use *your* butter spreader or dinner knife to spread it on the bread.

Don't re-dip a chip or vegetable stick into the dip. If you've taken a bite off it, that end may not go back into the common dip.

Don't put more on your fork or spoon than you can eat in one bite.

Don't make noise when you eat. Any sound, other than a crunchy veggie or an occasional moan of delight made while chewing is totally unacceptable. If your mouth is closed when you chew, then you won't have this problem.

Don't mix food on your plate unless it's meant to go together. Gravy over mashed potatoes, yes. But creamed corn and mashed potatoes, no. It may look good to you, but it probably won't to your fellow diners.

Don't reach across the table or across another person to get something. If it's out of reach, ask someone to pass it to you.

Don't pick your teeth in public, either with

DINING DON'TS
(Continued)

your fingers or a toothpick. It's pretty disgusting to watch. If you must, excuse yourself from the table and take care of the problem in the bathroom.

Don't lean back in your chair. As much fun as it is, it's murder on the chair and can be dangerous for you.

Don't flap your elbows like a bird flapping its wings when you're cutting or eating. Elbows should be kept close to your sides when you eat so you don't jab the person sitting next to you. If you are left-handed, ask to be seated at the corner with your left elbow out. It avoids a collision with your right-handed neighbor.

Dining Dilemmas

When do I start eating?
At a large party, you may start eating after three or four guests have been served. The hostess should say, "Please go ahead and begin," but if she forgets, pick up your fork and others will follow suit. In a group of four or six, it is certainly more polite to wait for everyone to be served.

*How do I serve myself from a platter or vegetable
dish with one big fork and one big spoon?*
Lift the food with the spoon and use the fork to
steady it. Replace the spoon and fork on the platter
side by side, far enough on it so there is no danger
of their toppling off. If the food is something that's
served on toast, such as creamed mushrooms, asparagus, or sweetbreads, slide the spoon under the
toast and lift the whole portion carefully—even
though you may not wish to eat the toast.

Which way do I pass the food?
When eating family style, food is passed from left to
right. If you are helping serve a formal meal, food is
offered from the diner's left side. Empty plates and
glasses are removed from the right unless that is
very inconvenient.

What if I drop a utensil on the floor?
When you drop a knife, fork, or other utensil while dining at home, pick it up, take it to the kitchen, and get
a clean one. In a restaurant, leave it on the floor and
ask for another. If it falls where someone might slip
on it or injure themselves it's safer to pick it up yourself, put it aside on the table, and ask for a clean one.

What if I drop food or spill something on the table?
If you drop a little food (jelly, peas, or a piece of lettuce) on the table while you're eating, scoop it up
with your spoon or the edge of your knife and put it
on the edge of your plate. If you have a small spill,

dab it with a little water to prevent staining and inform the hostess at the end of the meal. If you have a big spill, she'll know about it, so all you can do is apologize and help clean it up. If you're dining out and accidentally spill your beverage on the table, blot it with your napkin, then tell the waiter so it can be taken care of.

What if I have to blow my nose, cough, or sneeze at the table?
If you really must blow your nose during a meal, ask to be excused. It is unlikely you would have a tissue or handkerchief with you anyway, and we know you would never dream of using your napkin!

Turn your head and cover your mouth with your hand or your napkin when you sneeze or cough at the table. If the attack is prolonged, excuse yourself until it's over.

What do I do with seeds, bones, olive pits, etc.?
Small trash that occurs during a meal should be removed from your mouth discreetly with the thumb and index finger and placed on the bread and butter plate or the edge of the dinner plate. Larger objects—gristle, larger bones, skin—should be removed with the fork and placed on the edge of the dinner plate.

How can I eat the sauce or gravy left on my plate without scooping it up with a spoon?
Sometimes that sauce is too good to leave! Break off

a small piece of bread and put it into the sauce. With your fork, spread the bread around to soak up the sauce, then eat it. You may continue until the sauce or the bread is gone—but do it one piece at a time.

Where do I put paper packets from crackers, sugar, salt, and pepper?
They are placed under the rim of the dinner plate or on the edge of the bread and butter plate. In a restaurant, they could be placed in the ashtray, if no one is smoking.

What should I do when I'm dining at a friend's house and I finish eating before everyone else?
Join in the conversation until others are finished also; then you may offer to help clear the table. If your offer is declined, don't insist. If your offer is accepted, remove dishes from the right side of the diner. You may take two plates at a time to the kitchen, but never stack them.

Helpful Hints for Difficult Foods

◆ Artichoke leaves are eaten with the fingers. Pull them off one at a time, dip them in the sauce, and scrape them between your front teeth to remove the edible pulp. The "choke," which remains on the heart when the leaves are gone, is scraped away with your knife and the heart eaten with your knife and fork.

♦ Asparagus is often called a finger food, but unless it's very crisp, it's better, and easier, to eat it with a knife and fork.

♦ Chicken and chop bones may be picked up only when you're at an informal affair. Do it as neatly as you can after you've cut off as much meat as possible, and wipe your hands and mouth after each bite.

♦ Chicken nuggets, fish sticks, and french fries are finger foods when eaten as a snack or with other finger foods, but should be eaten with a fork when served as part of a main meal that requires the use of a knife and fork.

♦ Corn on the cob is messy, so just do the best you can! Butter and eat only two or three rows at a time so that you don't have the whole greasy ear smearing your hands and face. Use holders in each end if they are provided; otherwise it's strictly a finger food.

♦ Finger foods, such as sandwiches and corn on the cob, are obviously eaten with the fingers. Other foods that hold together well may also be eaten with the fingers: crisp bacon, bite-size portions of baked potato skins, fried cheese sticks, watermelon, or pickles, for instance. However, cake with soft icing as well as eclairs or napoleons, both of which have fillings that squirt when they're squeezed, must be tackled with a fork.

◆ Gravy is served with a spoon or small ladle, not poured from the gravy boat. Put it right over meat and potatoes or rice. Other accompaniments, such as jelly or relish, are placed beside the food they go with.

◆ Spaghetti is an Italian dish and should be eaten as the Italians eat it. A few strands are held against the edge of the plate (or large spoon, if provided) with the end of the fork, which is then twisted or twirled to wrap the spaghetti around the tines. When you have a nice neat coil, get as much to your mouth as possible and bite off the trailers. Don't suck up the ends with a loud slurp! If, after much practice, you just aren't able to master this technique, cut the strands and scoop them onto your fork.

◆ Olives, radishes, and celery go on the butter plate, if there is one; otherwise put them on the edge of your dinner plate. They are eaten with the fingers.

◆ Forks are usually provided for Oriental food, but don't be afraid to try the chopsticks. They are often presented in a paper package as two wooden sticks stuck together, but easily separated. Usually the top end is square and the bottom end is round. Use the round end to pick up food and put it in your mouth. The best place to put your fingers is in the middle of the chopsticks. Hold the upper one as you would a pencil—resting on your second finger and supported by your index finger. The upper half of the lower chopstick should rest on the juncture of your thumb and index finger, and the lower half on the end of your ring finger. The lower chopstick stays still and the upper one moves, but to work properly the two ends must be even and not crossed. Success takes practice, but it can be great fun to learn with a friend!

◆ Pizza can be eaten with the fingers or with a knife and fork—it depends on the pizza! Use whichever method you find the least messy and the most efficient.

◆ Raw fruit such as apples or pears should be cut into quarters and the core should be removed before the fruit is eaten with the fingers.

◆ Each shrimp in a shrimp cocktail should be eaten in one bite, using the cocktail fork. If the shrimp are jumbo size, you must cut them with the edge of the fork, keeping a firm grip on the shrimp cup with the other hand. When shrimp are served in a stemless bowl or on a plate, you may use your knife to cut them.

Dining Out

Fast food restaurants are the ones you are probably most familiar with and comfortable in. You wait in line for your order to be taken, and you clean your own table when you leave. When you're with a lot of friends, you may have a tendency to act silly or get a little rowdy. It's OK to have fun, but not at the expense of others around you. Be considerate of other diners.

Family-style and neighborhood restaurants are pretty informal, too, even though they usually have table service. If you use good table manners at home, you're not likely to come upon anything you can't handle here. When you're dining with friends, do be considerate of other diners, and don't forget to tip the waiter appropriately. (See "Tipping," Chapter 6).

Formal Date Dining

Teens usually feel the most insecure when dining with a date in a formal restaurant on a special occasion. To prepare you for any situation, let's run through an imaginary dinner date with Kevin and Caroline.

Kevin has been dying to ask Caroline for a date, so he calls her on Wednesday and asks her to go with him to the Snooty Pig restaurant on Saturday night. Caroline is really excited about going to such a special place with Kevin; she accepts the date.

Kevin knows that the Snooty Pig is a popular restaurant, so he calls several days ahead to make a reservation. He should be prepared to tell the reservationist what time he wishes to dine, how many will be in his party, and whether he wishes to be in the smoking or nonsmoking section. He may also add that it is a special occasion and he'd like a nice table.

When Kevin and Caroline arrive at the restaurant, Kevin lets Caroline out at the door and goes alone to park the car. Caroline waits just inside the restaurant door, and they go into the dining room together. If there were a parking attendant (or valet), Kevin and Caroline would both get out at the door and let the valet park the car.

Once inside, Kevin checks his coat, but not necessarily Caroline's. If she's carrying an umbrella she should check that, because it's a nuisance at the table, but she ordinarily would wear her coat to the table and drop the shoulders over the back of her chair when she is seated. However, if she is wearing a very bulky down or fur coat, she may ask Kevin to check it, too, remembering that he will have to add an additional tip when he retrieves both the coats.

If a headwaiter meets them at the entrance, Kevin gives his name and mentions that he has a reservation. Caroline then follows the headwaiter to their table, with Kevin walking behind her. If the table the headwaiter chooses is unacceptable because it's too close to the kitchen or the noisy waiters' station, it's OK to ask for a better one. Caroline is then given the choice seat—the one with the best view or the comfortable banquette against the wall. If they are both to sit on the banquette, Caroline waits for the waiter to pull out the table and slides in first. At a regular table, the waiter holds the chair for her, and Kevin sits down after she is settled. He may, but need not if it's too awkward, help Caroline off with her coat.

Ordering is Fun!

MENUS

There are two kinds of menus—à la carte and *table d'hôte*. An à la carte menu lists each item with a price beside it, and the cost of each item you order, including beverages, is added up to make your total bill. A *table d'hôte*, or "complete dinner," menu has a price beside the main course (often called the entrée) and then lists certain items—appetizers, soups, vegetables, salads, and desserts—with no prices. You may choose one item from each of these groups, unless the menu says otherwise, and the cost is included in the price of the entrée.

However, beware! There are almost always some items listed in these categories which do have prices beside them, and if they do, that amount is charged in addition to the price of the main course. Many "complete dinner" menus will say "Price of entrée includes vegetable, potatoes, and dessert." That means the price of anything else—soup, salad, coffee—gets added to your bill.

Table d'hôte dinners are usually less expensive than the same items ordered one by one à la carte, but remember that you must stay within the limits of what the menu says or the cost goes up!

Shortly after Kevin and Caroline are seated, the waiter brings their menus and takes their beverage order. They talk about what looks good, and what they are familiar with. Caroline asks Kevin what he's planning to have. His answer gives her a hint about how much he is able to spend. Unless Kevin says, "I'm having the chicken, but you order anything you want," Caroline should order something that costs approximately the same as, or less than, Kevin's selection.

In some really fancy restaurants, the woman's menu doesn't have any prices on it. It's preferable for Caroline to say, "My menu doesn't have any prices on it—help me make a selection." But if she's too embarrassed to say anything, she can order chicken or pasta instead of steak or veal, because they are usually less expensive, or she can order the same thing Kevin does.

When the waiter comes to take their order, he may mention some specials the chef is offering that evening that are not on the menu. If he does not mention the price of those items, it is appropriate to ask. Kevin and Caroline may also ask him to describe the zabaglione, gazpacho, or any other unfamiliar foods they have a question about. They may ask him to describe the soup and vegetables of the day as well; and if they are having trouble making a decision, they can ask the waiter for his recommendations. They should never be too embarrassed to ask questions about the menu. It's the waiter's job to answer questions about the food, and by asking, you make his work more interesting.

At one time women never spoke directly to a waiter but gave their order to their escorts. Seems pretty silly, doesn't it? If the waiter asks Caroline

---

SOMETHING TO REMEMBER ABOUT WAITERS AND WAITRESSES

As in all professions, there are some very good waiters and waitresses, and some very bad ones. The better ones are usually found in better restaurants. It is important that you remember that the waiter is there to serve you (even though sometimes they act as if they're doing you a big favor). This does not mean you should be rude or discourteous. It does mean you should allow the waiter to do his job.

For example, if you ordered a rare hamburger and you got one that was well-done, you should discreetly inform the waiter and have him bring you a rare one. If you drop your fork on the floor, leave it there and ask the waiter to bring you a clean one; that's his job.

For giving good service, the waiter should receive a tip equal to about 15 percent of the check, before sales tax. You give slightly more if the service has been special. You see, helping you is part of the waiter's or waitress's job. See Chapter 6 if you're unsure about tipping.

her selection it would be rude of her to ignore him and tell Kevin what she wants. So today she simply orders herself. Caroline doesn't have to order as many courses as Kevin unless she wishes to.

Enjoying the Dinner

When the waiter brings bread and butter or crackers, Caroline and Kevin should refrain from diving in as if they were on the verge of starvation. Gorging on hot bread and exotic crackers is tempting, but it takes the edge off the appetite for the better things to follow.

Table manners are the same in a restaurant as they are at home. The piece of silver farthest from the plate is the one used first, unless a special implement such as a cocktail fork is brought in with the shrimp or other appetizer. Bread should be broken into reasonably sized (not bite-size) pieces. If necessary, salad may be cut with a knife. Meat is always cut off the bones, and the bones are not picked up with the fingers. When the portion served is more than you can comfortably eat, it is acceptable to ask for a take-home box.

If Kevin or Caroline order something they have never seen before and neither one knows how it should be eaten, there's no cause for panic. (See "Helpful Hints for Difficult Foods," above.) No one else in the restaurant is likely to be paying attention anyway. So as long as Kevin goes slowly and doesn't make a mess of the table as he's eating the lobster, for example—and as long as Caroline doesn't break into hysterical laughter watching him—the difficulty should pass unnoticed. It's also acceptable to ask the waiter how to manage, but if you don't want to do that, you should just attack the food in the neatest way you can invent.

Time to Go

After their delightful dinner, Kevin asks for the check. While he is going over it mentally (not with a pencil and calculator), Caroline may choose to excuse herself to go to the ladies room. Although she could reapply her lipstick at the table, she should not comb her hair or do any other makeup repairs there, and Kevin will probably appreciate time alone to take care of the check.

If Caroline doesn't know where the ladies room is, she need not hesitate to ask the nearest waiter; he is asked the same question at least a dozen times a night. If there is a rest-room attendant who provides a service such as a clean towel, hair spray, or hand lotion, Caroline is expected to leave a tip of 50 cents, or even $1 in a very posh restaurant, in a little dish that will be positioned in an obvious place.

When the waiter returns to Kevin with the change, Kevin picks it up and leaves the tip. Fifteen percent of the bill is still the accepted tip everywhere but in the most luxurious restaurants or for extraordinary service. To figure it quickly, take 10 percent of the total and add half of that amount. Or if you live in a part of the country where sales tax is 7 or 8 percent, doubling the sales tax gives you a good estimate of the correct tip. If Kevin is using a credit card, then the waiter fills in a subtotal, leaving the space for the tip blank. Kevin fills in the amount, totals the bill, and signs the check. The waiter gives Kevin one copy of the credit slip and keeps the rest.

Kevin helps Caroline into her coat, and holds her chair or pulls the table away so that she can get up easily. They both make sure that they haven't left anything at the table; thank the waiter if he is nearby; and leave.

If the check says "Please pay cashier," Kevin would leave the tip on the table and he and Caroline would stop at the cashier's desk to pay the check. If he did not have the correct change for the tip, he would return to leave it on the table after getting change from the cashier. On the way out, they retrieve Kevin's coat from the checkroom, and he deposits 50 cents to $1 in the plate.

Special Situations

Kevin and Caroline's dinner was a very easy and pleasant one—nothing horrible or embarrassing happened. And this is the way dining out generally is. Sometimes complications arise, but if you know how to handle an unusual situation, every dinner can go as smoothly as Kevin and Caroline's.

Sending Food Back

There are unfortunate occasions when something does go wrong. You find a fly in your soup or lipstick on the glass, or your rare steak arrives looking like shoe leather. Call the waiter and ask for another cup of soup or a fresh glass, or explain that the steak which you ordered rare is well-done. If the waiter doesn't cooperate, ask for the headwaiter or manager and explain the situation to him. You may reduce the amount of your tip or leave none at all. If the waiter has been really rude, don't go back to that restaurant. But don't ruin the evening for yourself and your date by causing a scene.

Greeting Friends

If you see a group of friends at a nearby table when you arrive, stop and greet them briefly. When you stop to chat you'll be cluttering up the passageway for waiters and other customers, so save those long conversations for another time.

Suggestions for Smokers

If one member of a couple smokes and the other doesn't, the smoker should ask permission before lighting up. Of course, you must be sitting in the smoking section of the restaurant. If your date doesn't mind your smoking, be careful that the smoke from a cigarette left in an ashtray doesn't drift directly into your companion's face or toward your nearby neighbors. Don't exhale the smoke in anyone's face, either; it's very annoying to a non-smoker.

When there is no ashtray on the table, ask for one. It is disgusting to put out cigarettes or drop ashes on the edge of a plate, in your saucer, or on the floor.

Applying Makeup at the Table

Although it is still considered acceptable to apply a little lipstick at the table, using powder or fixing your hair is not. If you must do a makeover, excuse yourself and go to the ladies room.

Going Dutch

One of the bigger dilemmas about going dutch is figuring out whether or not an invitation *is* dutch treat. For instance, "Let's meet for a pizza" is not necessarily an offer to pay, but "May I take you out for pizza?" probably is. If you're not sure, try to clarify, by the least uncomfortable means, before accepting. Your response to "Would you like to meet me for pizza?" might be a lighthearted, "That depends on who's treating," or "I'd love to but I'm short on funds this week—how about a burger instead?" Either response gets you the needed information and is certainly easier than being caught in a situation where you don't have enough money.

Once you and your friends have decided to go dutch, there are several ways you can handle the check. If the restaurant allows it, each person should order his own meal and get a separate check. Otherwise, appoint one person banker; he or she can figure the check and tip, divide it by the number of persons present and tell each person how much they owe. Be sure to notice whether the restaurant automatically adds a service charge (tip) for large parties—usually eight or more. If so, don't add the tip in again.

Unless there is a large discrepancy in the amount each person ordered, it's best to divide the check evenly. The one thing to avoid is that confusing and ridiculous situation where each member of the group tries to add up his or her share and argues about whose dinner costs a few cents more. The waiter goes crazy, the other patrons think you're too young to be out without a parent, and your own party ends up in a royal battle.

Dining Alone

At your age there probably aren't many times when you eat out alone, but sometimes it happens. Often people feel awkward about eating alone, but it really can be very nice. You can order what you want and eat at your own pace. . . no need to speed up or wait for someone else!

Ask for a table that you like, one with a view out the window or off to the side so you can feel less conspicuous. Take along a book, newspaper, or magazine; it's OK to read at the table when you're alone and it helps pass the time. Once you realize that most people are not paying any attention to you or feeling sorry for you, you can really enjoy the time alone.

Chapter

4

APPEARING IN PUBLIC

Until now we've been talking about your behavior
with the people you know best or want to get to
know—family, friends, new acquaintances. These
are people who matter to you, and you don't want to
knowingly hurt or annoy them. Others deserve the
same consideration. How do you know that the person you cut in front of in the movie line won't be
your new tennis instructor? How do you know that
the nerd sitting next to you in math class won't
develop a hot new computer game?

We're not suggesting you be nice to people you
don't know because of what they may be able to do
for you in the future. We're suggesting that you consider all the facets of the people around you, and try
to see their good points instead of just what's annoying you about them at the moment. We're asking
you to consider how your behavior affects those
around you and how it influences what those people
think of you, whether or not you ever become friends.

Appearance

Think for a minute about someone you saw today, someone you didn't know, and what kind of impression they made on you based on their appearance. If you saw a woman in a white uniform and shoes at the grocery store, you probably assumed she was a nurse, though she may have been a waitress. If you saw a spastic young teen in a wheelchair with little control of his limbs, you might also have assumed he was retarded; but many victims of cerebral palsy have above-average intelligence, and all the feelings and emotions that any teen would have. More subtle impressions might be that the kid with the pocket protector and the lace-up shoes is a nerd, while the guy in the leather jacket and tight jeans is "cool." Not necessarily.

We use these examples to help you understand that how you look and act influence what people think about you until they have a chance to know you better. Take a look at yourself and see if you're sending the signals you wish to send.

Posture

Posture is part of your image as well as dress. If you are dressed appropriately for a job interview yet you sit across from the interviewer leaning back in your chair, eyes wandering around the room, he has the impression you are not interested in what he has to say, nor in the job. Maybe you're not. But if you are, you would sit straight or perhaps lean slightly forward in the chair, and look the interviewer in the eye as he speaks.

Lots of teens slump, sometimes because they feel they're too tall, sometimes because they think it looks cool, sometimes because they don't think. Slumping gives the impression that you don't feel very good about yourself, that you're trying to shrink or disappear. Even if you feel that way sometimes, try standing up straight—and you really will feel more confident.

If you catch yourself slumping, here's a quick remedy: Pull yourself up as if you were a puppet with a string coming out of the very top of your head; then raise your shoulders and try to touch them to your earlobes. Get as close as you can, then let your shoulders drop. This is the natural position for your shoulders, not thrown back. Try to maintain your "string" as you walk and sit.

Public Spaces

Places that you frequent—shopping malls, health clubs, public parks, pools, golf and tennis facilities—are frequented by adults and children as well. It's important to keep that in mind when you use these spaces. For example, a sign spotted recently at the entrance to a shopping mall read:

> RULES OF CONDUCT
>   No loitering
>   No offensive language
>   No excessive noise
>   Proper attire required
>
> Failure to comply with the above "Rules of Conduct" will result in suspension from mall property.

I doubt that many of the teens to whom the sign was addressed had even noticed it, but the mall office confirmed that Security had used the posted rules as a reason to suspend from the mall teens who were not obeying them.

There are similar signs at pools, parks, health clubs, and sports facilities—places where people, when having a good time, tend to forget how their behavior affects others. Pay attention. Don't embarrass yourself by being asked to leave a public facility because of your appearance or behavior.

What to Do When

There are times when you're out in public and unsure as to what is the right or wrong thing to do. For example, what should you do when. . .

. . . The elevator doors open?

When the elevator is crowded, the persons

closest to the door exit first. When it is uncrowded, it's polite to let women and girls enter and leave the elevator first. The person closest to the "Door Open" button should hold it until everyone is through getting on and off the elevator.

. . . Entering a revolving door?

If the door is already moving, the woman traditionally steps in first while the gentleman pushes from behind. If it is stationary, he steps in first and gets it moving while she steps into the section behind him.

. . . Going through a pull door?

Look around you when you approach a pull door. Is there someone behind you with an armful of packages? Is there a young mother with a stroller? Is there an infirm or handicapped person with a cane or wheelchair? If so, pull the door open for them, and let them pass ahead of you. Well-mannered men also step aside and hold the door open for women. When there is another person a step behind you you needn't let them go ahead of you, but it's courteous to hold the door as you go through rather than just let it close behind you.

. . . Going through heavy push doors?

As with the pull door, look around you. Go through the heavy door first, but don't let it slam until you've checked to see if you can be of help by holding it for someone coming behind you.

. . . You feel the urge to write on bathroom doors and lunchroom tables?

You know what they say, "Fools' names and fools' faces always appear in public places." Graffiti, or the destruction of another's property, is also against the law.

. . . You've finished your meal and there's no trash can nearby?

Hold on to your litter. In many states there is a stiff fine for littering. Think, too, about how you feel upon arriving at your favorite picnic spot to find the remains of someone else's meal.

Public Performances

People who attend movies, concerts, sports events, and plays usually pay good money to see a performance that will provide them with a few hours of enjoyable entertainment. Why, then, do they often behave in a way that prevents their fellow audience members from doing the same?

Haven't you ever had a movie ruined by someone sitting nearby and talking; or a formal concert made miserable by an inconsiderate person in front of you who whispers throughout the performance; or a sports event spoiled by a poor loser cursing and screaming; or a play where you missed the initial plot line because of late arrivals climbing over you to get to their seats?

Make sure you're not one of those people who ruins a performance for someone else. And if someone else is ruining yours, try some of the tips in "Talk About It," in Chapter 1. For example, to the person talking at the movie, say, "I can't hear when you're talking. Would you please be quiet?" If that's ineffective, you can move or go get the manager. There are times when it is appropriate to let someone know how their behavior is making you feel.

When Playing Sports

There is no question about it—being good at sports is an asset to any young person. But more important than being a good athlete is being a good sport. Some of the worst public behavior you'll ever see happens during sporting events. Please remember these points:

◆ Temper tantrums are immature and very unattractive. What do you think about someone who breaks a tennis racquet, throws a golf club or baseball bat, or argues with a referee?

◆ Do your best and play enthusiastically. Everyone likes to play with someone who appears to be having a good time.

◆ Don't make lots of excuses about your mistakes and don't dwell on your errors. A shrug of the shoulders and "I'm sorry, guys" will do.

◆ Be sincere. Comments such as "Oh, that's too bad—you almost made a hole in one" will seem insincere to your opponent. It would be better to say, "Doesn't it make you mad when you miss a close one?"

◆ When you win, give the loser a handshake and a positive comment. A good winner, no matter by how wide a margin you won or how poor a player you consider the opponent, should try to convince the loser that it has been a good match. If the winner can help the loser think he or she has played a good game and was fun to play against, he has succeeded in being a winner that everyone can applaud.

◆ When you lose, give the winner a handshake and a sincere "You played well." Swearing at your luck, making excuses, complaining about conditions, and, worst of all, protesting a decision by a referee or umpire get you nowhere except into trouble. Of course luck can be a factor; but in general, you lose because on that day you play an inferior game, and the test of a good loser is being able to accept the loss and act as if you enjoyed the match and played your best. You must be sincere in your congratulations.

Just remember that no matter which sport or sports you enjoy, you will have a better time and be more in demand as a partner or opponent if you show consideration, enthusiasm, and good sportsmanship.

When Traveling

When you're traveling alone, it doesn't really matter how loudly you play the car radio or how many clothes you leave around your motel room. But when you travel with others you must be considerate of them.

- ◆ Plan ahead. Allow yourself plenty of time to think through what you'll need, pack it, and show up at the appointed departure time so that *you* aren't the reason the plane or bus is missed.
- ◆ Be prepared to entertain yourself. Take games, books, snacks, or handwork—anything to help pass the time on a long trip. Pay attention to airline rules about electronic equipment during takeoff and landing.
- ◆ Be quiet. If you don't have earphones, play your music softly, and talk only if those around you seem receptive.
- ◆ Be still. Squirming in your seat, kicking the seat in front of you, turning lights off and on, and general restlessness can be very annoying to those around you. In hotels, jumping on beds, slamming doors, playing on elevators or escalators, or running up and down the halls are similarly annoying.
- ◆ Be considerate. Bathrooms on planes and buses can get pretty grungy unless each passenger does his part to leave it clean. Be sure you flush the toilet, drain the sink, and put your trash in the appropriate container.

◆ Be safe. Keep your seat belts fastened at all times.

Graduation

This is an incredible milestone in a teen's life. Sometimes you expect so much out of this one occasion (the ceremony, the special date, the dance, the breakfast) that you are exhausted and disappointed when it's over. Some pointers for a memorable occasion:

◆ Plan ahead. Visualize the kind of evening you'd like to have, then work toward that goal. Would you like to have your grandparents travel across the country to attend? Let them know at the beginning of the year and see if it can be worked out. Do you want to rent a limousine for your special evening but know your parents would never spring for it? Call for rates early in the year, then get a job or save your allowance, or get a few friends together and split the cost—or decide it's not worth it and find an alternative.

◆ Study. You can't graduate if you don't pass. It's really hard to keep working when the end is in sight, but it's worth it.

◆ Include special people in your life. Due to the size of many graduating classes, many schools limit the number of people students may invite. There can be problems with broken families— both parents may want to attend, but don't get along—or there aren't enough invitations to include the neighbor who looked after you every day while your Mom worked. Make time to do something special with those you can't invite—have a celebration lunch with your stepdad, or write a note to your neighbor telling her how much her support meant to you and how she'll be with you in spirit.

At the same time, don't err in the other direction: Send invitations or announcements *only* to those who are close friends or relatives. It's tacky to send lots of invitations just to get gifts.

◆ Knock out the grunge work. You enjoy getting gifts and notes of congratulations, but don't feel like addressing the announcements or writing the thank-you notes? Too bad! If someone cares enough to choose and send a gift, you *must* thank them for it.

As an upcoming graduate, certain behavior is expected of you—maybe not what you had in mind, but you need to be aware that it is expected. You are to. . .

Show up for graduation rehearsals, and pay attention.

Knowing when it's your turn to go on stage and how to shake the principal's hand while accepting the diploma can keep you from making a fool of yourself.

Dress and act appropriately.

You know what we mean. Your school has laid out the rules. Don't *you* be the one who ruins the occasion for others.

Respect other people's property.

Just because someone has been nice enough to host a graduation party doesn't give you permission to "trash" their house or grounds as part of your "celebration."

As the guest at the graduation of a friend or relative, you are expected to do as any good guest would:

Let the graduate know whether or not you will attend the ceremony or function to which you've been invited.

Send a gift or note of congratulations.

Arrive on time, dressed appropriately.

Don't embarrass your friend during the ceremony by screaming his name or throwing confetti. You may appropriately stand and clap as he receives his diploma.

Bar Mitzvah

A Jewish boy's bar mitzvah closely follows his 13th birthday. It is a deeply religious occasion celebrating his acceptance as an adult member of his congregation. The ceremony, which may be lengthy and elaborate, is usually followed by an open gathering in the social rooms of the synagogue, and may be attended by anyone wishing to offer congratulations. There is usually a more elaborate private party later in the day to which relatives, close friends of the parents, as well as friends and classmates of the boy are invited.

If you are invited to attend a bar mitzvah, it is important that you attend the ceremony as well as the party. Your friend has prepared long and hard for the ceremony and it is a very meaningful part of his life. Whether you are Jewish or not, you may find it an impressive tradition. You should dress appropriately for both occasions, so it would be a good idea to check ahead of time with someone who might know what the occasion calls for.

Usually, a gift is sent to the young man prior to the ceremony. A gift of $18, called *C'hai* (meaning "to life") money, carries a lovely sentiment. Or you may choose to give $36, signifying a wish for "double life." Clothing, stationery, or a religious article are also appropriate.

The *bat mitzvah* is a corresponding ceremony for 13-year-old girls in some Conservative and Reform congregations. It may not be as prevalent or as elaborate as a bar mitzvah, but the same guidelines would apply.

Debuts

A debut today is certainly not what it was 40 years ago, when it was marked with elaborate balls and entertainments and served to announce a young lady's introduction into adult society as well as her availability for courtship and marriage.

Today's deb is usually a recent high school graduate or has just completed her first year of college. She will most likely be presented with a number of other young ladies at a large ball sponsored by a charity organization or assembly. Most of the parties honoring her prior to the ball are hosted by a group of friends and may honor several other debs, as well.

As a guest at a party or ball, you are expected to:

Respond promptly to any invitation you receive. It is most rude to cause a host to incur additional expense because you couldn't take the time to send regrets.

Dress appropriately. If you're not sure what to wear to a party or ball, call a hostess or someone who has previously attended such events.

Act appropriately. Most debs are not of legal drinking age but their escorts and guests may well be, so alcohol is available at many of their parties. If you are underage or don't know your tolerance for liquor, this is not the time to indulge. Getting boisterous or sick as a result of too much booze is an embarrassment for you and your family, the hosts, and the honoree.

Surprisingly, a gift is not traditional nor expected at debut parties or balls. If you are really good friends with the deb and want to do something for her, a small remembrance—jewelry, fragrance, a blank book or photo album—given prior to the ball would be appropriate.

Weddings

Presumably, we're not talking about your wedding here, but one that might include you—perhaps that of a close family member or friend. Whether you're invited to take part in the wedding or simply attend parties, showers, or the ceremony, it's important to remember that these are celebrations honoring the bride and groom. It's their special time, but one that can sometimes be stressful because of all the plans and decisions to be made. Honor them by doing your part to make events that include you run more smoothly.

Chapter

5

SOCIAL SURVIVAL

What do *you* have to do with *your* social survival?

Everything. Believe it or not, *you* are the one making the choices about how, and with whom, you spend your time. And *you* are the one who will ultimately have to take responsibility for the choices you make.

You will absolutely feel pressured by your peers to do certain things—some of which you'll want to do, and some of which you won't. There is good peer pressure: to make good grades, to look attractive, to wash your car often. There is not-particularly-good peer pressure: to date at an early age, to go steady, to attend parties you don't especially want to attend. And there is bad peer pressure: to use drugs and alcohol, to smoke cigarettes or marijuana, to shoplift, to have sex for the wrong reasons.

Some teens give in to the pressure in order to

feel accepted. Great, if it makes you work harder for good grades, but not so great if it makes you get drunk every weekend. Other teens give in to the fear of not belonging by refusing to be pressured, which is great if it keeps you from shoplifting, but not so great if it has you making C's when you could be making A's.

Think about the times you feel pressured. Ask yourself why you feel you need to go along with the group. We all want to be liked, but do you really want to risk being arrested for smoking pot just to get someone to like you? Is this really the type of person you want for a friend?

Remember that you always have a choice and you always have the right to say no. You don't have to do something that someone else wants you to do, especially if it doesn't feel right for you. When you make a choice you accept responsibility for your action. *You* are the person with the power.

What You Can Control

Your Health

You can't control whether you get the latest flu virus or common cold, but you can do a lot to stay healthy.

Exercise
One of the most important things you can do to

clear your head and re-energize is to exercise. If you're an athlete, then you may get enough exercise already. But if most of your exercise is walking from your room to the kitchen, you need to do more. Find an activity you like—biking, Rollerblading, walking, tennis, golf, weight lifting, swimming, or working out to an exercise video—and *make* yourself do it four times a week for a month. After that, it'll be a habit—and one you'll feel good about.

Sleep

You'd probably *love* to have more sleep, but your activities keep getting in the way. Getting up early for school, late sports practice, after-school job and homework, hanging out late with friends, watching your favorite late-night TV show, weekend chores and errands—the list of excuses to stay awake is endless. But your body needs rest. And when it doesn't have it, it takes to bed with an illness. Make a healthy choice to make time for sleep.

Diet

Eat right. No doubt your diet is packed with fast-food burgers, fries, pizzas, and tacos. There *are* times when nothing else will do. But there are also times when you're just too lazy to do anything else. In the same restaurants, and for about the same amount of money, you can choose healthier alternatives. There are also "fast" foods like fresh fruit, popcorn, and fruit juice available at groceries and delis which can add some healthy variety to your diet. Check the nutrition information each restaurant provides, and learn to read labels. You'll be surprised at what's healthy and what's not.

Eating Disorders

How you look has a lot to do with how you feel about yourself, and how you perceive others feel about you. Be realistic about your body. Nobody likes every part of themselves, and there's definitely a time in late adolescence—just before your period starts, or you begin to get hair under your arms or on your chest—when everybody looks chunky. It's a hormonal thing over which you have no control. But you do have control over how you let it affect you.

Look at pictures of your babysitter or an older sibling when they were 12 and when they were 17. See the difference? Some things just get better with age. In the meantime, do your best to look your best, but don't go to the extremes of bingeing or purging unless you're willing to *die* to look better. If you think you may have an eating disorder, ask for help. Tell an adult you trust, or check the phone book for a crisis line or eating-disorder hot line. (See "Calling for Help," in Chapter 1.)

Sexually Transmitted Diseases, AIDS, and Pregnancy

You have control over whether or not you get yourself into a situation where you feel pressured to have sex. You *can* avoid those situations. Usually alcohol or drugs are involved with teen sexual experiences, because they reduce your inhibitions. You can choose to stay alert. You can make conscious choices.

If your choice is to have sex, do protect yourself. Condoms are easy to obtain and can prevent disease and pregnancy. If you're too embarrassed to buy or use one, picture how embarrassed you'll be when your friends find out you're pregnant, or that you're dying of AIDS. It happens to people every day who thought it would never happen to them.

Your Activities

Though you may not feel it or realize it yet, you are special. You have a gift that no one else has. Whether it's the ability to make people laugh or the smarts to understand complex mathematical formulas, it's your gift to find and develop. Spend some time focusing on your uniqueness, and involve yourself in activities to enhance it.

Constructive activities that you can use to enhance your life and fill your time include hobbies, music, church groups and trips, leisure or competitive sports, fashion, academics, volunteer work, or school groups, clubs, and activities.

Destructive activities, which are so prevalent in the lives of many teens, are against the law—and can have long-range consequences. We recently read of a teen who shoplifted a tube of lipstick "for kicks." She was caught, fingerprinted, and booked. She realized her mistake and has changed her ways, but now that she's filling out job applications she has to answer "yes" every time she's asked if she's ever been arrested. The "kick" wasn't worth it, but she didn't take the time to think of the consequences.

Activities that can get you into big trouble are underage drinking, driving while intoxicated, using illegal drugs, using a fake ID, vandalism or graffiti of another's property, possessing a gun, crashing a party, stealing or shoplifting, having sex with a juvenile, forcing a date to have sex with you (date rape), or having an illegal abortion. Now that you've read this, you can't pretend you didn't know.

Popularity

What makes one teen popular and another not? That's a really hard question to answer—it varies from town to town, school to school, and sometimes from week to week in the same school. But in most cases, the teens who are popular seem to have qualities that others admire, and they *seem* to feel confident at a time when many of their peers do not. There are things you can do to develop your best qualities and build your confidence, but they still don't guarantee that you'll be voted homecoming king or queen.

To put things in perspective realize, too, that the majority of your peers are *not* popular. The "in" crowd is a small percentage of your class, so there are lots of other places for you to be happy.

We know of a teen who tried very hard to work his way into the "in" crowd, and for a short time he was able to do it. But, wisely, he realized that he had very little in common with that group. He didn't enjoy their company or activities. He could fake it to stay "in," but he chose to go back to his former friends—a nice, middle-of-the-road group of guys.

He chose to stay in the background, until one day his best friend signed him up to do a drum solo in the high school talent show. The rest of the class had no idea how much time this teen spent with his drums. On the night of the talent show, he took first place while his classmates screamed his name and begged for an encore. It was a moment every teen dreams of. He wasn't elected homecoming king, but he'd found his unique talent and his confidence—and it opened the doors for college scholarships and a lifetime hobby.

Friendship

Though you may not be the *most* popular, you will never be *un*popular if you know how to be a good friend. A friend is. . .

Trustworthy. If you've ever been betrayed by a friend you thought you could trust, then you realize the value of trust. Make sure that what is said to you in confidence remains confidential, no matter how juicy it is. There is absolutely nothing to be gained by betraying a trust, and there is much to lose.

Loyal. If you care about someone, then you need to stick by him or her in the bad times as well as the good. After all, you'd expect the same.

Involved. You can't be a friend without becoming part of another's life, and making that person a part of yours. Friendships require time and attention, but the rewards are great.

Dating Data

Twenty years ago, dating rules were much clearer. Girls never called boys for dates—only boys could call girls. Girls never paid for dates—boys always did. Girls never opened their own doors or pulled out their own chairs—boys did it for them. Group dates and dutch treats were rare. It's probably the way your parents, and most adults you know, dated—which may help you to understand why they don't understand your dating habits.

Obviously things were a little lopsided then, but the advantage was that one knew what to expect. Now you have many more dating options, but you have to communicate clearly—there's no more certainty about who asks, who pays, etc.

Showing Your Interest

Times have changed, and it is no longer the boys who must initiate social activities. This takes some of the pressure off the guys and gives the girls an opportunity to develop friendships, as well as dating relationships, with boys.

Neither boys nor girls like to be harassed by someone to whom they have politely made it clear they are not interested. If someone avoids your calls or makes excuses for why he or she can't see you or talk to you—take the hint. Remember, the fact that someone is not romantically interested in you doesn't mean they don't like you at all. Give them some space.

So how do you know what's enough and what's too much? How do you go about expressing an interest in that certain guy or girl? Begin by treating others the way you'd want them to treat you.

- Be your best—be the type of person people want to know. Look attractive, and be active.
- Be honest, but be kind. Your best friend just dyed her hair green and asks if you like it. If you hate it, try to refrain from saying that you now know what Martians must look like. Instead, tell her what you liked better about her regular color or style: "Green is definitely different, but I liked your hair better when it was red."
- Don't gossip or betray a confidence, or talk about others behind their backs. It can be hard not to go along when others start to gossip, but

think how you'd feel if you learned others were talking about you behind your back.

◆ Smile and speak. Never be afraid to speak or say hello to anyone. Are you ever offended when someone speaks to you? Maybe you feel shy or are afraid that by speaking to that "certain person" he'll know you like him. If you smile and say hello to everyone, then no one person can feel they've been singled out and everyone just thinks you are friendly. Play a little game: Make yourself smile and greet the people you pass in the hallways at school. Before long it will be a habit, and there will be a new, friendlier you—one whom other people will want to know more about!

◆ Be interested. *Listen* when others are talking to you and take an interest in what they have to say. Don't just pretend to listen when all you're really doing is waiting for them to stop talking so you can talk again.

◆ Develop common interests. If he's in the business club, maybe you could join too. If you know she plays tennis after school each day, schedule a game on the adjoining court. Join church, school, or community organizations of which he is a member. The more often you run into each other (without being too obvious, of course), and the more interests you have in common, the better the chances for a relationship to develop. But don't forget to remain open to meeting others with common interests rather than just focusing on one person.

◆ Arrange a meeting. If the love of your life has a class with one of your good friends, arrange for your friend to introduce the two of you. You might also have your friend arrange a blind date, or invite you both to a small party.

◆ Introduce yourself. If his hall locker is right next to yours, or if you run into her often at the swimming pool, there's no reason why you can't introduce yourself. After talking for a minute or two, you'll have a better idea of what your chances are. Grumpy, one-word replies aren't very encouraging, but cheerful, enthusiastic conversation should give you the courage to get to know one another a little better.

Asking for a Date

If you think, after you've met and talked, that he or she might be interested in you, why not ask for a date? We realize this is not always as easy as it sounds, but here are a few tips to make it easier:

◆ Ask early. Two to four days ahead of time is sufficient for a regular date, earlier for a special occasion. You're more likely to be accepted if the person you're asking doesn't feel that they're unpopular or a second choice. Exception: A group of friends decides to go out for pizza or a movie at the last minute, and you think your new "friend" might fit in. Call and ask him or her to join the group. Dutch treat. No strings.

◆ Call or ask in person. Don't send a note through

a friend or have someone else ask—it looks as if you're afraid or don't have the confidence to do it yourself. Also, if you get turned down, you'll be glad no one else knows!

◆ Use good timing. Don't ask for a date when she's talking to a group of friends, or when he's in the middle of basketball practice. And if you want to make an impression on his or her parents, it's best not to call at the dinner hour or after 10 P.M.

◆ Be specific. Never ask, "What are you doing Saturday night?" Instead say, "Would you like to go to the movies Saturday night?" Once you've been accepted, be sure to give the time ("I'll pick you up at seven"), the transportation ("We're double dating with Paul and Diana in Paul's car"), and what to wear ("It's pretty casual—I'm wearing jeans"). If you have a curfew, be sure to mention it: "Is it OK if we go to the first feature? I have to be home by 11:30."

◆ Be clear about who pays. An invitation to go out doesn't always mean that the person doing the inviting is paying. If you're doing the asking and you're planning to pay, say something like, "I'd like to treat you to Putt-putt and a pizza Friday night. Are you free?" If you can't afford to pay but want to initiate the date, say something like, "I'm short on funds but I'd love to go dutch for a burger before the football game Saturday night. I can drive. Would you like to go?" If you've been invited out and you're not sure who's paying, you can say something like, "I'd love to go out with you. Do you want to go dutch treat?" Or you can just take enough money with you to cover your share if you need to.

◆ Start slowly. If you're still getting to know the person and you're not sure you're ready for four or five hours alone, plan something that lets you hang around together, talk, and decide if you want to spend more time together. You want a chance to get to know each other better without spending too much time or money. Perhaps you could invite her to fly kites one weekend afternoon, or you could invite him and another couple over for pizza and a game of Trivial Pursuit. Sharing study time or working together on a school project is another good way to begin.

If the answer is yes. . .

Be enthusiastic and excited when accepting a date, or don't say yes. If you can't give an immediate answer, state why: "My parents aren't home from work yet and I have to check with them. Can I call you back in an hour?"

Once you've accepted the date, you must keep it unless you become ill or a family situation requires your presence. If you wish, you may suggest another time.

If the answer is no. . .

Be honest about your refusal. If you're holding out for a better date, simply say, "I'm really sorry, but I already have plans." Then the person who asked you out won't be surprised if he sees you at the movies with another guy (or girl), or finds out you stayed home with your parents.

Refusing a date you'd really like to accept requires sincere regret so you'll be asked again. If the reason you must refuse is mentionable, give it: "Oh Scott, I'm *really* sorry but this is my weekend with my Dad and he's made plans. I'd love to go out with you another time." That's a reason that *is* true, *sounds* true, and opens the door for another date.

If someone you aren't interested in dating persists in asking, it's probably better to tell him how you feel gently and honestly than to lead him on indefinitely. Just say, "You know, I don't think I'm the person for you, but I'm really flattered that you asked."

Think before you refuse a date. After all, a date only lasts a few hours, and you might really like each other. If not you don't have to go out again.

If you do refuse a date, for whatever reason, keep it to yourself. Don't tell all your friends so they can have a good laugh behind his back, and don't tell Amy that the only reason she has a date with Scott on Saturday night is because you turned him down. Just remember how you'd feel if someone said those things about you.

Dating Dilemmas

Sometimes it's really hard to solve a problem when you're right in the middle of it—you just can't be objective. The basic rule of etiquette, to treat others the way you'd like to be treated, can help solve many of the dilemmas of dating. Remember, though, that treating others the way you'd like to be treated doesn't mean you always do what someone asks of you. It means being true to yourself, but mindful of the feelings of another. You'd be surprised how many tight situations you can get yourself out of by answering, *honestly*, "How would I want to be treated in this situation?" Then act accordingly.

Blind Dates

For some reason, blind dates are usually considered dilemmas—"Should I go or not?" You wonder, "If he or she is so cool, why don't they already have a date?" A blind date may seem a better option than sitting at home, but you usually expect it to be a bore.

If you can tell in the first five minutes that you have nothing in common, suggest a movie where you won't have to talk much, and use the date as an opportunity to practice your charm. Keep in mind, though, that we actually *know* married people who met on a blind date!

Going Steady

Like everything else in life, going steady has its pros and cons:

Pros	Cons
You don't have to worry about dates.	You're out of circulation.
You can feel at ease.	It can be boring.
You get to know each other better.	You get too involved.
It proves your feelings for one another.	You feel pressured to have sex.
It makes you feel attractive.	It ties you down.
Everybody does it.	Everybody does it.

Think about it. Breakups aren't easy. So before you say yes, be sure you're doing it for the right reasons.

Breaking Up

It's very rare that two people want to break up at the same time, so usually one person ends up getting hurt. There's really no way to avoid that, but there are things you can do to make the pain a little easier.

You'll be tempted to end it with a note or a phone call or a disappearing act because it's easier, but don't. Tell your steady that you need to "talk" about something important, face to face. He or she will know something's up and have a little time to prepare. Maybe by the time you meet, your steady will realize breaking up is the thing to do. If not, at least there's a chance to ask questions and try to understand what went wrong.

Realize that there *is* real pain attached to love, so it's understandable that you feel hurt over a breakup. Express anger if you need to—pound your pillow, stomp your feet, have a long talk with your best friend—but be careful what you say and to whom. Remember, you really cared about this person once. An outward appearance of "It was great fun but it was just one of those things" will get you over the hump and back in circulation.

Sex

It seems that sex is everywhere; advertisers use it to sell everything from toothpaste to cars, songs are written about it, and movies show all. It's no wonder that some of you think sex is no big deal. *Think again.* Sex is meant to be an expression of love between two people who really care for each other. It's giving a part of yourself to another. Not something to do because:

- ◆ "Everyone else is doing it."
- ◆ You want to prove to the guys how hot you are.
- ◆ You don't want to be a virgin anymore.
- ◆ You want to know how it feels.
- ◆ You want to be accepted or loved.
- ◆ Your steady is pressuring you.
- ◆ You think it's the only way to hold on to the relationship.

Girls usually equate sex with love; so if she has sex with you, she's likely to expect more from the relationship. Are you ready for that?

Before you make a decision to have sex, ask yourself these questions and answer them *honestly*.

- Is everyone else really doing it—or are they just talking a lot?
- If I have sex with this person, will I be able to look him/her in the eye tomorrow and talk about the sexual experience openly?
- If it doesn't go well, how will I feel—embarrassed, angry, hurt, used?
- How will I feel if we break up afterward anyway?
- Am I willing to buy and use a condom?
- What if this experience results in pregnancy or disease?
- Do I really trust this person?
- Do I like/love this person?
- Is this the *only* way to prove my love?

Statistically, most teens who had sex at an early age regretted it. In retrospect, they realized they did it for the wrong reasons—and the experience would have been better if they'd waited to share it with someone they really cared about.

GREAT DATES

- Monopoly, Trivial Pursuit or Pictionary
- Miniature golf or a driving range
- Rollerblading
- Picnics in the park
- Hiking
- Flying kites

GREAT DATES
(Continued)

- Horseback riding
- Swimming
- Ice skating
- Fairs, carnivals, circuses, rodeos, and horse shows
- Music or poetry reading at a coffeehouse
- Museums and art galleries
- Dancing: Fast, slow, line dances, or Western dancing are all great fun if you know how. If you don't, lessons can be lots of fun too.
- Local plays or musical presentations
- Classes, lectures, seminars, and demonstrations, especially in college towns. Try a Chinese cooking class, karate demonstration, or a lecture on nature photography.
- Church activities: You don't have to be a regular churchgoer to enjoy many of the activities planned by church youth groups.
- Renting a video, making popcorn, and inviting another couple to watch the film with you.

BAD DATES

- Parking in a deserted area
- Field parties
- Crashing a party
- Cruising or joy riding

BAD DATES

(Continued)

◆ Sneaking into a bar or club
◆ Rented hotel rooms
◆ Hanging out in the bad part of town
◆ Partying at a deserted beach

Parties and Proms

Parties and proms feel like incredible milestones in a teen's life. Sometimes you expect so much out of one special occasion that you are exhausted and disappointed when it's over. Visualize the kind of evening you'd like to have, then work toward that goal, but be realistic about your expectations. For a memorable occasion think about:

Your date:
Ask early for big parties and proms. Girls need time to choose a special dress, and guys need to reserve a tuxedo.

Your transportation:
Do you want to rent a limousine for your special evening but know your parents would never spring for it? Call for rates early in the year, then get a job or save your allowance, or

get a few friends together and split the cost—or decide it's not worth it and find an alternative.

Your driver:

If you don't have your license yet, try an older sibling or friend. Some kids rent buses and vans, which come with a driver. If you or one of your friends decides to drive, make a commitment to *stay sober.*

Your budget:

Big evenings get expensive. Save your money and think of ways to economize. Dinner before the dance at someone's house can be less expensive than a fancy restaurant. Take your own party pics at the dance rather than springing for the expensive ones. Get creative!

Flowers:

It's often a school custom to exchange flowers for special dances and proms. A boy should ask his date the color of her dress and order flowers that will complement rather than clash with it (your florist can really help you make a good choice). Wristlets (a corsage with an elastic band that can be worn around the wrist) and nosegays (a small bunch of flowers to be carried) are more popular than corsages, which must be pinned to the dress. If you do opt for a corsage, it can be pinned at the waist, high on the shoulder, or even on an evening bag.

HOW TO PIN ON A CORSAGE OR BOUTONNIERE

Remember that a corsage or boutonniere should be worn with the flowers up, the way they grow. Insert the pin into the fabric of the dress, back up through the fabric and over the stem (about the middle of the corsage), then back through and out the fabric. Corsages sometimes come with two pins so you can criss-cross them to hold the flowers more securely. This requires some practice. You may want to get some help from your Mom or an older sister before you try it on your date.

A young lady usually presents her date with a boutonniere, or small flower for the lapel, usually a rose or carnation. If she plans ahead she can even get a flower to match the corsage she'll be wearing. She pins it where the buttonhole would be on the lapel of his jacket by holding the flower in place, inserting the pin into the fabric, then up through the fabric and flower stem, back into and out of the fabric.

Before the Dance

It's customary to go to dinner before a prom or dance. It doesn't have to be the most expensive restaurant in town. As we mentioned earlier, it can be very nice and a money saver to have dinner in someone's home. Maybe the girls would like to cook for the guys, or someone's parent would really enjoy doing so.

If you do go to a restaurant in a large group, try not to disturb the diners around you by celebrating too loudly. Also, be aware that many restaurants automatically add a service charge (tip) to the check for parties of eight or more. Check your bill before you add the tip.

At the Dance

Someone went to a lot of trouble to plan the dance, decorate the room, and hire a band or DJ. Too often, teens stay long enough to get their picture made, then move on to other parties. Try staying at the dance a while. You may find it fun.

After-the-Dance Parties

If no private home is offered for an after-the-dance party, your group may come up with some unsafe or illegal alternatives. *Use your common sense.* If you're picturing an evening where you celebrate by getting drunk and getting laid—think again. The reality is that getting drunk often leads to getting sick, passing out, or serious automobile accidents—rarely does it lead to a wonderful evening. And getting laid often leads to an unwanted pregnancy, sexually transmitted disease, AIDS, or at the very least, with such high expectations, a disappointing sexual experience. Be aware of what the group plans are and try to suggest a safer alternative than the beach, all-night clubs, or rented hotel rooms.

Concerned parents at some schools schedule all-night parties, such as a "casino" where teens win play money which they then use to buy donated items at an auction. Pool parties are also popular—followed by a breakfast, of course.

Curfew

Most teens do have a curfew, but usually it varies depending on the occasion; you get to stay out later on weekends than weeknights, later for special parties than regular dates. We hope that your parents discuss the time with you and that your curfew is a reasonable one. There will be times when you run late for reasons that can't be avoided—your car has a flat, the movie runs later than expected, or the party doesn't end on time. As soon as you realize you will be late, call your parents and explain the circumstances. If you aren't late too often, they'll probably be helpful and understanding when you are.

MANAGING YOUR MONEY

Most teens feel they never have enough money. As a matter of fact, most adults feel that way too! What can you do to have enough?

Where It Comes From

Allowance

Most teens get their spending money from an allowance. The ideal amount is one that covers all of what you need, but not all of what you want. Sorry, but if the purpose of an allowance is to teach you how to manage money in the real world—that's it. There are ways to supplement your allowance or earn money for the things you want.

Gifts

Unfortunately, gifts of money can't always be counted on. Most often, they come as surprises. You should never ask for money, but if you are approached for a birthday, Christmas, or Hanukkah suggestion, you may say something like, "I'm saving up for a new sound system, so money would be helpful." It's also OK to tell your parents you'd like cash in case they are asked for a suggestion.

Jobs

Most teens we've known who *really* wanted to earn extra money and were willing to work have been able to find or create a job for themselves. This is definitely the best way to increase your income while making you feel really good about yourself. Job specifics are given in the next chapter.

Borrowing

This is *not* the best way to get extra money. Creative borrowing can help you budget, though. We know of a couple of college students who work and share an apartment. Because of their pay schedules, one of them has more money at the beginning of the month, while the other has more money near the end. So one "borrows" from the other by letting the first person pay bills that fall due at the beginning of the month, then "pays back" by handling the bills at the end of the month. They take their responsibilities seriously, and they trust each other to pay their share. As a rule, you should borrow only when it's absolutely necessary and when you're sure you can pay it back promptly.

Student Loans

Many college students get through school with the aid of student loans. The application process is lengthy and involved, and the amount you are awarded depends largely on your family's income, but it is worth the effort to get an education. If you are a high school student planning ahead, look into the many types of loans available. Realize, though, that the money is usually paid at the beginning of each semester; it will take some serious money management on your part to make it last until the end. Most students supplement the loan with a part-time job.

How You Manage It

There are a number of ways to manage your money. You may choose only one, or a combination of ways depending on your expenses.

Cash

Cash is the easiest to manage. When you have it, you have it; when it's gone, it's gone! It's not wise to handle a large amount of money this way—you don't want to have a lot of cash on you or stashed around your room—but it is by far the easiest way to handle "fun money."

Checking and Savings Accounts

As an adult, much of your money will be managed through checking and savings accounts. The sooner you can learn to write a check, balance a statement, or earn interest on your savings, the better understanding you will have of money management. Some banks will not open a personal checking account to anyone under 18; others require that you be 21 to have your own account. If, however, you apply at a bank where your family does business, and your parent or guardian is willing to sign for you, most banks will open an account for you. You will very likely *need* a checking account when you begin college, so it is wise to get a little practice before that.

Automatic Teller Machines (ATMs)

Some people put their money in a checking account and never write a check. They take all of their money out through an ATM and handle transactions in cash. For small transactions (buying CDs, cosmetics, movie tickets), this is fine, but for larger transactions (rent, phone bills, a new guitar), checks are preferable. Unless you are very careful to keep written records of checks and withdrawals, you can easily overdraw your account, resulting in expensive service charges. Treat your ATM and your credit card with respect.

Safety note: Do be alert when using an ATM. If someone seems to be lurking nearby, go to a different machine. Don't crowd the person ahead of you. Have your card ready and do your transaction quickly. Never flash your cash or cash card.

Credit Cards

Perhaps your parents let you use one of their credit cards from time to time as a matter of convenience. They may want you to have it in case of an emergency, in which case you should use it *only* in an emergency.

If the card is given to you for a specific purpose ("Go buy your school supplies") and for a specific amount ("Don't spend over $40"), then you must stay within the limits your parents have set. When you're not the one who has to pay the bill, using a credit card may seem like getting something for free—but your parents do have to pay up and they know their budget. It would be thoughtless of you to run up charges they did not authorize and may not be able to afford. If you misuse your parents' card you may find it won't be offered to you in the future.

Credit card companies target recent high school graduates and some college students with mailings aimed at getting you your own credit card. They will make it very easy for you to get one. You can get into big debt, though, if you don't use the card wisely. Use it for convenience, and not to buy things you can't afford. If you don't have the money in the bank, you won't be able to pay the bill. A bad credit record in college can follow you for life, and make future credit and loans difficult to get.

Where It Goes

Whether your money comes from an allowance, a job, student loans, or any combination of the above, you need to be very clear about what you are going to spend that money on. If it's just fun stuff like snacks and entertainment, then you may only need to save up for an occasional big date or special present. If, however, you are responsible for big items like rent, utilities, phone bills, clothing, a car loan, and insurance—and if you also wish to belong to a health club or tithe to your church or put aside some savings—then you will need to plan ahead. There are good books at the library on managing your money. Check them out!

Tipping

A hidden expense that we often forget about is tipping. Some teens don't realize that in many jobs (waiter, cab driver, hairdresser), the major part of an individual's income comes from tips. Others think that, because of their age, they do not have to tip. Should a waiter be penalized because he has been assigned to wait on you? Is it fair to expect the same service that an adult would get if you are not prepared to pay at the same rate?

Admittedly, the practice of tipping occasionally gets out of hand, and there are times when you can refuse to tip—namely, if the service has been really bad. But if it has been good, teenagers, like everyone else, must accept the responsibility of paying for it.

If you are ever in doubt about whether or not to tip for a particular service, watch those around you and follow their lead. There may be some variations according to where you live, but generally the following rules apply.

Waiters

15% of the bill before tax in most restaurants; 20% of the bill before tax in a more formal restaurant or for exceptional service in any restaurant; 10% in a buffet-style restaurant where you serve yourself except for beverage, bread, etc.

Some restaurants automatically add the tip (also called gratuity or service charge) to your check, especially if you have a large party. Be careful that you don't tip twice.

Headwaiter

$5 if he rearranges tables to accommodate your group or performs other special services. Tip him when you leave the restaurant. No tip is necessary if he simply shows you to your table and hands you the menu.

Room service waiter

Check the room service menu when you order to see if a service charge or gratuity will be included in your bill. If it is, no further tip is necessary. If it is not, tip 15% of the bill (but no less than $2). You may tip in cash or write it on the check.

Checkroom attendant

Even if there is a charge for checking your coat, tip the attendant. If no charge, tip 50 cents per coat for more than one coat, but $1 for one coat only. No extra tip for packages unless there are many.

Washroom attendant

Tip 50 cents to $1 if she does nothing more than hand you a towel, $2 if she does more. If the attendant does nothing more than look at you, no tip is necessary.

Strolling musician

Tip $1 for playing a request, up to $5 for several, no tip if you don't make a request.

Lunch-counter attendant

No less than 25 cents if you order only a beverage. Otherwise tip 10% of the bill (but no less than 25 cents).

Pizza or other takeout delivery

Tip $1 and change to $2, depending on difficulty of your

order and distance of delivery, up to $5 for a large "pizza party" order.

Valet parking attendant

Tip $3 in large cities, $1 to $2 in smaller cities. Tip when he brings the car when you leave.

Shoeshine

Tip 50 cents for shoes, $1 for boots.

Taxi drivers

Tip 50 cents for a fare up to $2, 15% of a higher fare.

Airport porters or skycaps

Tip $1 per bag.

Hairdresser

Tip 15% of total bill; likewise for waxes, facial, and manicures. Tip the shampooist $1.

Chapter

7

JOB DATA

So you want to earn some money. How do you go about it? Where do you begin? Whom do you talk to?

Some states require you to get a work permit, often called "working papers," when you are under a certain age. Your guidance counselor or school office may have all the information and application forms you'll need. If not, check the federal and state laws with your local Labor Department office. You'll also need a Social Security number. Since parents must report the Social Security number of all their dependents over the age of 5 on their federal tax returns, you may have a number and not know it. Ask your folks. If you don't have one, you can apply at any U.S. post office.

The younger you are, the more creative you may have to be about your employment—some businesses are just not going to hire a 14-year-old, no matter how responsible you are.

Check Your Resources

Have you ever worked before? Perhaps you haven't worked for pay, but you probably have some experience that you can market. You may have mowed your own lawn for several years; why not begin a neighborhood lawn-maintenance service, or consider working for a nursery or landscaping service? Maybe you've been baby-sitting since you were 13; why not do a summer camp for neighborhood kids at your house, or look into employment with a day care center or a local summer children's program?

Maybe you've taken classes that could be helpful to you in getting a job. Can you type? Do you know computers? How are your filing and bookkeeping skills? Do you know anything about car repair? Can you drive?

Think about your interests. Do you like to meet people? Can you cook or garden, sew or knit? Do you like selling? Are you interested in caring for the sick or elderly? Do you like reading, or drawing, or calligraphy?

When you've really thought about your talents and abilities, you may have some idea of what kind of job you'd like. The next step is to get ideas from other sources.

◆ Talk to your parents. They know you best and will have helpful ideas about what you'll enjoy and be capable of doing.

◆ Network. Consider as potential employers parents of your friends, friends of your parents, or a business where you are a regular customer—a grocery, clothing, music, or video store.

♦ Discuss your interests and abilities with your school counselor; they are often aware of job opportunities for teens.

♦ Check the classified advertisements in your local newspaper. Large companies and private individuals often find employees this way, and you may see something that appeals to you. You'll also notice that employment agencies advertise in the classifieds. If you get a job through an agency and the ad doesn't say "no fee," there will be a charge—usually a percentage of your first month's or year's salary—so you may want to consider this as a last resort. Look for ads that say "no fee" before considering those that do charge a fee.

♦ Community bulletin boards. Usually, there are bulletin boards at local businesses in your neighborhood. Consider advertising your services there.

Prepare a Resumé

Finally, after you've explored your options but before you've contacted potential employers, prepare a resumé—a history of yourself. It should be prepared on a typewriter or word processor so it looks good. If you can't type get someone to do it for you. It should include the following information:

- Name, address, telephone number
- Social Security number
- Education—Diplomas or certificates received, if any, or last grade completed
- Honors or awards you received in school
- Courses related to the job you're applying for
- Interests and hobbies, especially if pertinent to the job you're seeking
- Past work experience, if any
- Names, addresses, and phone numbers of three people who would be willing to provide references. You may choose from previous employers, members of the clergy, teachers, and family friends, but before listing them, you *must* get their permission. You should not give family members as references.
- If you have a good recent professional or school photo of yourself, it is helpful to include it. Snapshots should not be included.

Check your public library for more resumé specifics, and for books on different types and styles of resumés.

With all the preliminaries out of the way, you must now decide whether you want to work for someone else or for yourself. Each choice has advantages and disadvantages. First let's investigate working for someone else.

Setting Up the Interview

Start Early

If you're looking for summer or after-school and holiday employment, these are peak times and employers have many applicants from whom to choose. If you're ahead of the crowd, you'll be more memorable.

Some job sources that are popular with teens, such as fast-food restaurants and grocery stores, do not require you to make an appointment for an interview. They usually conduct interviews at set times—Tuesdays and Thursdays between 2 and 4 p.m., for example. You can either pick up an application ahead of time and take it with you to the interview or fill one out when you go. (Note: It's a good idea to pick up several different applications ahead of time so you can look them over and practice filling them out. Take your scratch copy with you to the interview, and you'll be sure to have all the information you need if you're asked to complete an application on the spot.)

Other businesses, such as department stores, take applications at any time. You simply go to the personnel department at your convenience, fill out an application, and meet with a personnel officer for an interview.

Most of the time, though, you are expected to call or write for an interview.

Calling is easy—simply phone the personnel office, give them your name, and tell them that you'd like to set up an appointment for a job interview. You should then be given a date and time to appear.

Classified ads often give a post office box to write for an interview, rather than a phone number. If you wish to make a good impression on a prospective employer, your letter must be neatly typed or written and must include all pertinent information.

The Interview

Now that you have an appointment with your potential employer, remember to:

Dress Appropriately
Be sure your hair and nails are clean and well-groomed. Your clothes should also be clean and pressed. For an office or store job, a boy makes the best impression in slacks or trousers (not jeans), a shirt and tie, well-shined shoes or loafers, and a conservative sports jacket. If you're applying for a construction or landscaping job you may wear jeans and a workshirt, but they must be clean and neat. A girl looks best in a nice skirt and blouse, suit, or tailored dress, hose, and shoes with medium heels (like something you might wear to church). Makeup and hairdo should not be too extreme nor clothes too tight.

A good guideline is to choose an outfit that is

slightly dressier than what you would wear to work at the job for which you are applying.

Be on Time
You don't make a very good impression if you're late. When you arrive, go directly to the receptionist and state your name and the time of your appointment with Mr. Personnel. Then sit down and wait patiently until you are called.

Take Your Resumé
Even if you are asked to fill out an application, your resumé will have needed information such as the addresses and phone numbers of references and your Social Security number. Never go to an interview without this information. If you are a legal immigrant, bring proof of citizenship. While you may not need it when you are first interviewed, if you are hired you will need proof of citizenship before you can begin work, so it is not a bad idea to have it with you.

Remember Your Manners
Approach the interviewer with a smile and a firm handshake. Remain standing until you are told to sit; then sit in the chair indicated or one that is across from the interviewer. Even though you may be nervous do not chew gum, smoke, or fidget.

Be Prepared
Let your interviewer direct the conversation, but when the lead is turned over to you, be ready with

some intelligent questions about the training program, opportunities for advancement, and the work you would be doing. If you are applying for longer than a summer job, you may also ask about vacation time and pay, but only *after* you are sure you are interested in the work itself.

Remain Calm

Of course, this is easier said than done, but you'll make a better impression if you do. Sit comfortably in the chair but don't slump, and look your interviewer in the eye when you speak. Don't swing your leg, tap your feet, wring your hands, or do anything that gives away how nervous you are.

Be Honest

The importance of honesty cannot be overestimated. Lying to make yourself look good can cost you your job if it is discovered. Also, many employers ask potential employees to undergo a lie detector test.

Thank the Interviewer

You can do this enthusiastically when you leave; you can also follow up with a short note thanking the interviewer for his or her kindness.

Working For Yourself

Maybe you will not be able to find employment because of your age or schedule. Whatever the reason, here are a few self-employment suggestions to consider:

- Lawn service—mowing, edging, weeding, or gardening
- Child care—regular baby-sitting
- Delivering newspapers
- Neighborhood newsletter—Sell ads to local businesses and get news from local residents, then publish weekly or biweekly.
- Services to the elderly—reading aloud, writing letters, or running errands
- Pet watching—caring for pets for people who work or are out of town. Contact local veterinarians for referrals.
- Fix toys and bikes
- Wash and wax on wheels—Go to places of business or homes to wash and/or wax cars.
- Cake or cookie baking—for any occasion
- Disc jockey for parties
- Plan parties for children—Assist the parents, or accept full responsibility for the party.
- Small painting jobs—Paint fences, doghouses, patio furniture, garage doors.
- Typing or computer work
- Gift-wrapping service—your home or theirs
- Ironing—Pick up clothes, prepare them for pressing, iron them, and return them to the customers.
- House sitting—Check on houses for people who are out of town; turn on lights, water plants, bring in newspapers, feed pets.

◆ Errand service—Run errands for people in your neighborhood.

As you can see, there are lots of things you can do; but you must inform people of your service. Let them know by phone, community bulletin board, flyer, or postcard.

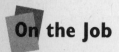On the Job

No matter what type of job you do, to be successful you must do it well. Be prompt. Be enthusiastic. Be cheerful. Be conscientious. Be courteous!

INDEX

ABOUT THE AUTHORS

Elizabeth L. Post, granddaughter-in-law of the legendary Emily Post, has earned the mantle of her predecessor as America's foremost authority on etiquette. Mrs. Post has revised the classic *Etiquette* five times since 1965. In addition she has written *Emily Post's Complete Book of Wedding Etiquette*, *Emily Post's Wedding Planner*, *Emily Post's Advice for Every Dining Occasion*, *Emily Post on Business Etiquette*, *Emily Post on Entertaining*, *Emily Post on Guests and Hosts*, *Emily Post on Invitations*, *Emily Post on Second Weddings*, *Emily Post on Weddings*, *Please Say Please*, *The Complete Book of Entertaining*, with co-author Anthony Staffieri, and *Emily Post Talks with Teens About Manners and Etiquette*, with co-author Joan M. Coles. Mrs. Post's advice on etiquette may also be found in the monthly column she writes for *Good Housekeeping* magazine, "Etiquette for Everyday."

Mrs. Post and her husband divide their time between homes in Florida and Vermont.

Joan M. Coles is an etiquette consultant from Baton Rouge, Louisiana, who taught manners and etiquette at the Emily Post Summer Camp.